All the pain
—*and*—
*suffering made
me stronger*

All the pain
— and —
suffering made
me stronger

CRUZ PATIÑO

Library of Congress Control Number:		2013902853
ISBN:	Hardcover	978-1-4633-5071-0
	Softcover	978-1-4633-5070-3
	Ebook	978-1-4633-5069-7

This book was printed in the United States of America.

Revision Date: 04/05/2013

To order additional copies of this book, contact:
Palibrio
1663 Liberty Drive
Suite 200
Bloomington, IN 47403
Toll Free from the U.S.A 877.407.5847
Toll Free from Mexico 01.800.288.2243
Toll Free from Spain 900.866.949
From other International locations +1.812.671.9757
Fax: 01.812.355.1576
orders@palibrio.com
439646

Chapter 1

I want to tell my story to help others. I do it like an auto therapy for myself. I'm from Ecuador from a little village named Sinicay. It all began from my childhood when i was six years old, i lived with my mom and dad in a mud house with my two brothers and two sisters i was the youngest. My family and I worked on making bricks. We were very poor but united as a family; we often had no food and went hungry.

On one occasion we ran out of clay to work my parents made the decision to go to the east of Ecuador, they thought we would do better by going east, with hard work my parents were able to buy land in

Sucua, Ecuador it was a beautiful place full of fruit trees and livestock. My mom had to go from one place to another because my brothers stood back home because I was the youngest i accompanied my mom wherever she went. She used to take me between her legs, I felt loved and happy. We ate oranges, cassava, papayas and other fruits. We had cows that we would milk and take fresh milk from and make cheese to go sell the next day with my sister. We were about 30 minutes from where we lived so we would manage to sell and then bought some things we would need.

Everything was wonderful despite being poor and humble. On one occasion walking in the countryside, my brother and I saw a clump of papayas. My brother and I could not resist the temptation to eat the delicious fruit. However a snake bit my brother's leg i screamed in terror to see how my brother was rolling in pain i thought he was going to die. I started screaming even more and asking for help. My sister and a boy appeared to help and later on my mom came. They took my brother to Sucua I did not stop crying, my mother consoled me by hugging me and told me that everything was going to be okay. Three days of anguish worrying have passed and finally my brother was ready to leave the hospital and return home with us. My parents decided it was best to return to Cuenca but Rocio had decided to keep her baby in Sucua. My dad had gotten use to living in Cuenca because of his habit of drinking aquardiente *(alcohol distilled from sugar cane)* he drank more and more and more each passing day.

Flor the youngest of my sisters found a job at a small restaurant in Sucua. So she decided to hide from us so she won't have to return to Cuenca with us. She fell in love with a boy named Sergio and had decided to live with him. We had to go back to work making bricks. My parents had to buy land for clay, we had to work very hard and early sometimes we had to rest till late at noon we only had about 20 minutes to rest; although I was a child I had to learn how to work, I did not study, my parents had no money, I just had the chance to finish second grade. Unfortunately that was normal for us there was no other way of life but work. My childhood turned into the workplace, making bricks, sweating all day, tiredness, joys and tears.

Chapter 2

My father began to drink heavily every day that went by and we did not know the reason why, my sister Flor decided to stay in Sucua and my mother and I worked very hard, my family began to change and fall apart, my father was no longer the same he was very aggressive with my mother. I missed my loving father who spoiled me and gave me advice. But when he drank alcohol he was very different. I really was scared and on several occasions I would hide under the table.

My sister Rocio came back to Sinincay with her baby, she became a single mother and came back to live with us. My brothers Rafael and Antonio also worked hard with us to help Rocio. My Father and Rocio got along very well, but I clung to my mother more. Over a year or so, my sister Flor came back to Paute near Cuenca. We had searched a long time and after much questioning, from here and there, we finally found where she lived. When we found her she would not return to Sinincay she had decided to stay in, since there was her husband. About eight months after returning to live with us, she was expecting her first baby, we all lived and worked together, had problems because of my sister loved Flor and Rocio and not always been so. Rocio always been the one, she wanted all the attention and sought to win any situation, no matter who was hurt with her personality, Flor and Sergio were married and before the birth of her baby, he had made a small house near the house where we lived, they moved in their house to avoid problems with Rocio, but at home the situation did not change Rocio fought with my brothers, and lied all the time, and her baby was very spoiled by my father. She said that I did not give her food. Sugar, or anything else, to make my father mad at me, my brother Rafael cannot stand watching the situation and the needs we were going through he raised money and with hard work he was able to buy a truck Ford 600. I remember it well, because for me it was the best thing we had experienced, the truck would help us work because we made the bricks and now we could sell it in many more places.

Thanks that we had that truck, we could go out to the coast to buy bananas and resell. We sold vegetables and fruits. My family was very loved by others; a family who had a farm near us gave us the opportunity to work on their property, making bricks, glasses, ceramic plates and cups so we could sell in Cuenca.

One morning my father went searching for firewood in the furnace bricks, Flor and I were with one of my aunts and my brothers were with mom at the factory, My mother and my brothers saw my father as he entered the house and quickly changed into different clothes and went out but gave no importance or explanation, that day changed my life completely, my mother and my brothers were surprised to see the arrival of one of my father's nephews he looked very worried. He brought bad news that my father had died on the way. My mother and my brothers were quick to see what had happened, my sister Rocio went to my aunts house with great sorrow and gave her the bad news that my father was dead, my world flipped i felt a sharp pain i could not believe my father was dead. I wanted to see my father because i could not believe what they were saying; I did not accept the fact that he was dead Flor did not want me to go she wanted me to stay to help clean the house because we had to have a place to bring the body. Later on they brought the body of my father and put him on the floor on a mat that was woven.

All that Passed through my mind was the memories between him and me I recode each of his advice he had always told me, be good, take care, and one of the most surprising for my age, that I would never fall in love with a married man and to not destroy any marriage. Those were his last advice as if he was going to die. The next day he was taken to a hospital for an autopsy i did not know what that was, and would rather not know, i have not yet accepted the fact of being without my father I preferred him drunk, but alive but nothing could be done it was a very bad time for me, I felt useless, decayed, I only had his memory, the Dr. gave us the results and what surprised us was that my father did not die because of drinking, he died of a disease called siticircosis which was an animal that lived in the brain that had consumed the blood like a worm, It had consumed all the blood and that's why he died. Dr. explained that liquor had calmed him from the unbearable pain caused by the disease. And at the time if he had cured it he would have been better. We did not know of his illness we did not know it was very painful for him, after three days we gave him the last goodbye, we were all missing him, I suffered a lot, there was a moment where I wanted to jump into the tomb with him in the Pantheon.

Our lives changed completely. My brother Rafael had already planned his wedding for some time and had already made preparations long before my father died. A month after my father died he got married.

I woke up one night, I had a dream that i was playing with my father, my mother asked if I was ok and she told me that he had gone to heaven and from there he took care of us and that god took him to be with him. I felt a little relieved, but still I really missed him a lot. Deep inside me there was a part of my father and his love that would never die and always would live in me, even though he's gone . . .

Chapter 3

As days passed, the owner's brother began making his farm and offered us to work there. Mr. Alberto also gave me work in spite of me being nine years old My job was to plant trees, flowers, roses, apple trees, eucalyptus, cypress and more. For me it was fun, i did not play like other children, so that kept me entertained, throwing down shovel to make holes in the dirt. I started to dream that one day these trees would grow very tall. We kept making bricks; we would stop only when it rained because it was very difficult to work in such conditions. The year my father died my sister Rocio got married, my mother and my brothers helped her make a house so that her and her husband along with her son can live together. Problems did not stop, my brother Rafael went to live with his wife's parents. All that was left were me Antonio and my mother; I liked being on the farm as Mrs. Maria the wife of the dr. gave us food to eat and on the weekends also gave us extra money. What I would do is give the money to my mother. I neverminded that the work was hard but what hurt me was that my family was falling apart; I missed the days when we were all together.

My sister Clara gave birth to her second baby, back in that time it was tradition to take care of the mother and new born for the first forty days. Miguel was the husband of my sister and had gone home and asked my mom to send me so i would take care of Clara his wife and also to take care of the their other child and to do housework such as doing laundry, making food. Although i was ten years old I was given a adults obligations.

They lived in a little mud house and the kitchen was like in a basement. I went with the intention of helping my sister, far from knowing what to expect. I was cooking chicken soup and hot chocolate for my sister and the kids when Miguel scared me as he entered and closed the door and went against me i was terrified he tore my clothes and started kissing me everywhere. He began to touch my body and raped me . . . I could not defend myself, he was to stronger and he RAPED ME, He took advantage of his strength. He threatened me and mocked me telling me that "No one will believe you, nobody will believe you, and if you tell your going to be responsible of what happens to your sister" he screamed in my ear. I felt very dirty i immediately ran to my mother's house before getting to the house i got some water to wash the blood still running down my legs. I wanted nothing to be left of that awful moment. I could still feel the warm blood running down my legs and pain and helplessness I felt. I got home and slept I did not want to tell mom.

The next day, that cursed man came back like nothing happened and had the nerve to ask my mother again if I would take care of his wife and children. I did not want to go, but my mother forced me. For the second time that damned man raped me. He had returned from work earlier than usual. He came to the kitchen and locked me inside again, this time my mother was looking for me and calling me. He heard outside the house. I was glad to hear her voice. He threatened me warning me not to say anything and that if I said something it will be worse for me. I was full of fear I thought how could my sister live with this monster.

I thought why this had to happen to me, cursing the damn man. On the third day, he came back again to ask my mother if i could help take care of his wife, I did not want to go. My mother got really upset with me and wanted to force me to go; I was shaking and did not know what was going to happen. So I told my mother what he had done to me and that he had raped me twice. But what surprised me was that my own mother did not believe me. In that moment I missed my father so much he would have believed me and not left me alone. I ran out desperate to an unknown path I ran and ran crying with rage. I sat next to a tree. I was hurt at the fact that my own mother didn't believe me; I thought she cared about me; I wanted to die at that moment.

An aunt who was returning with her animals saw me crying and grieving and approached me very concerned and asked me what's wrong? Through tears, I told her what happened with Miguel; I could not take so much pain and wanted someone to know. She was in rage and anger she went to leave her animals and then went to see my mother to talk to her. My mother and aunt fought, my aunt yelled how was it possible, she believed that damned man than her own daughter they discussed a lot, my mother insulted my aunt saying she was a nosy person, and to not meddle in our lives and she knew what to do and what not to do with her children.

From that moment in me started to grow resentment towards my mother. From that moment I tried to work far away as possible from my mother i was trying to get away from her and that horrible man, I would have nightmares about what had happened to me and constant fear would come over me. My mother had failed me, when there was work far away i would take it, on other occasions i worked hard with my brothers making bricks. On the weekends I would go to Dr. Alberto farm and worked. I worked to try to forget and not think about what had happened to me, my life had changed forever because of the sick mind of that man.

Chapter 4

My sister Flor and her husband Sergio had problems. Sergio would drink alcohol and became very violent towards my sister, Andres their son was only two years old and on one occasion Sergio got very drunk and came home and started to beat Flor, we were sleeping at that time when my nephew Andres came running to us very scared, crying and screaming that his father was beating his mommy. We got up and ran out to see what was going on. I got very angry wanting to defend my sister as I tried to force him off of her, he reached my finger and bit down on it. He bit me so hard that I wanted to cry of the pain I was in and scream of pain. He let go of my finger and ran, I cried of pain as i saw my finger almost falling off my hand. My sister and brother took me to some lady's house where she healed the wound and cleaned but I kept bleeding a lot so they took me to the hospital. Arriving there they stitched my finger, i went back to the home for about a month I could not do anything my sister would help me comb my hair, she would dress me and bathe me. I would see my nephew Andres sadness when I was sobbing, i told him that it was suppose to hurt but it was healing, as time went by we continued to work making bricks and returned to live together again. Dr. Alberto had good ground for making bricks. We had to buy some land from others to make bricks making bricks was our life, our work. Sergio returned around eight months later and apologize to my sister, she accepted his apology and they reconciled and started to live together again. Later after a while, Sergio and Flower started to work with us my brother Rafael had gotten an extra job as a truck driver he was getting paid per day and delivered bricks to others in Cuenca.

Chapter 5

When my brother's wedding occurred Rafael friends, family and acquaintances attended the celebration, my brother's wife, had a nephew named Rosendo and we met there. We danced and talked at the party and said, we wanted to get to know each other more; we made a date to see each other next Sunday. But I could not see him that day because he had gone to see his aunt, he had gone to see me but I would hide from him I was terrified i did not know what to do he was a man, I was afraid everything ran through my mind and that awful moment when I was raped i thought what happened if he was the same and that maybe he would do the same thing to me as that awful man did. I went out for a walk, I went to my aunt's house she asked me what did i want i replied and told her i was hiding from a boy. She began to listen to me and asked me "Why?" i told her i was scared of him finding out what had happened to me and that maybe he would stop liking me. My aunt gave me some advice and told me, it was better that I told the truth because he would find out sooner or later. Throughout that week I was with this anxiety i could not be still.

Sunday had arrived and he accompanied me at one point we were alone I found the courage to tell him what had happened to me and how awful I felt. Rosendo heard me out and told me that he didn't care that he still loved me but just wonder if my mom knew what had happened to me I told him yes but she did not believe me, he hugged me and told me he loved me, that he didn't care about anything else. I felt calmer hearing his words, we began a relationship we were together for almost a year, and we kept our relationship a secret for some time until people began to notice. His mother opposed to our relationship because according to her i came from a poor family. Mrs. Bernarda thought my family and I were paupers and that i was not good enough for her son. I had almost turned eighteen and me and Rosendo decided to run away from our houses, we went to a house of a woman named Monica, The next day the truck wouldn't start so Rosendo went looking for a mechanic, I was worried because my mom did not know that we were together our plan was to go first his parents and tell them we were getting married.

But everything went wrong, before coming to the workshop, his mother saw him, she found him and put him in a taxi and I was left alone not knowing what to do I went back to Mrs. Monica for to helps I explained what had happened and she took me back to my house. My mother was looking for me, Mrs. Monica was taking a long time speaking with my mom but finally i was home again i did not hear about Rosendo for about four or five months, until one of his friends came looking for me and told me that Mrs. Brenarda had sent Rosendo to the United States to go meet up with the father who was already there, She wanted to separate me from Rosendo and she finally did, she didn't care about me and Rosendo and the love that we had. Rosendo's aunt came to the house and told me that the day before Rosendo had traveled to the United States. She told me that he would try to contact me, I felt shattered, I loved him and it hurt me a lot that he was away from me. One of his friends approached me, his name was Eduardo, I spoke with him and he told me that Rosendo had said, he did not want to know anything about me, that he had played with me and mocked my feelings and that he would never had married me. I was destroyed i was so hurt, another heartbreak in my life.

Chapter 6

$\mathscr{I}$ spend much time with Eduardo after that had happened and he started treating me, as months went by a relationship started to grow between us two, we were together for about a year and half and more. We were ready to get married we started planning every detail. I started to accept the fact that I did not want to know anything about Rosendo anymore. But a new problem came along Eduardo's parents also did not accept me, it seems that love was not meant for me, we kept our relationship hiding. Time went by and I got pregnant I did not tell him anything yet we had sworn to get marry even though his parents opposed, everything seemed perfect, until one day i felt very bad he immediately took me to see a Dr. I was surprised that I was chosen first, I was thinking he was going to find out that I'm pregnant he walked into the room and asked the Dr. to give me some vitamins so I would not feel bad, The doctor pulled out a injection and gave it to me. I thought it was okay because there were vitamin injections back then so I kept quiet and after that i had to take one in two weeks again, Eduardo started to change he was aggressive, he would insult me and scream at me that he had played with me and he would never marry me, that he knew what my sister's husband had done to me, he said that the other day he had bumped into him and they started drinking and he told me that you would provoke and seduce him. I screamed he is lying he raped me! He told me that he would not marry a woman who messes with her sister's husband.

The terrible pain invades me. I wanted to die, but knowing that in my womb was a baby growing gave me strength to move forward, I hid it my pregnancy the best i could. I hid under my tummy under my apron, so my mom and brothers would not notice Eduardo, had planned to marry another woman, apparently he was afraid that I could ruin his plans. He did not want anybody to know that I was pregnant with his baby. A few days before his wedding, his sisters had gone to my house and started accusing and insulting me that I was trying to ruin their brothers wedding. They launched against me and beat me until I was lying on the floor. Eduardo denied being the father of my son, My mother had seen everything she found out about my pregnancy, she was furious and gave me a beating, I thought I was going to lose my baby she took a stick and still kept hitting me, My brother Rafael went to see my mother and began to defend me, my mother told him she was hitting me because i was pregnant. Rafael answered that my sister Rocio had done the same, but she did not beat her, but my mom did not understand. I decided to go live with my aunt, and four weeks later I went to live with my sister Flor, my baby was to be born Sergio and my sister took me to Cuenca. my sister Flor and Sergio and aunt accompanied me, I gave birth to a beautiful baby, I named him Jose like my Father. When the nurses brought me my baby i noticed he was carrying a tumor in the back and he was missing an ear i asked the Dr what was going on he asked me if i had taken any medication during my pregnancy i told him that the only thing I had taken was an injection of vitamins where Edward took me the Dr. shook his head and said they wanted you to lose your baby and that the injection was for abortions. He told me nothing could be done, I loved my baby, and I was grateful to God that he had survived. I had no money not a penny, how would i pay the medical expenses? All I had was a pig, I had agreed to sell it to my aunt and she agreed to buy it. So I could pay the bills, but i had no pampers for the baby, no clothes and with the little that I had left over from medical expenses, i went to buy the basics for my baby. I was alone and it was my first baby he had my last name . . .

Chapter 7

My mother appeared three days later and she was still very upset with me, she had come to see me out of obligation and not because she wanted to but because she did not like to be disturbed. I knew my mother I was surprised on how she was acting towards me. I never thought that my mother and my brothers would turn their backs on me in the time I needed them most. I went to my mother's house, but nothing was the same everything had changed, she was cold and very distant my brother Antonio was bothered when my child would cry he screamed and commanded me to shut him up. They were very unfair towards me and my child, as three months went by i had to baptize my child. I had my brother Antonio as the godfather, Rafael had advised me that I did so, so my mother and Antonio would fall in love with the baby, when my baby started to crawl, he would go towards Antonios legs and said uncle or Father cutting in words. They were slowly falling in love with my baby and that made me very happy, seven months later, my brother Antonio got married. They had a big party at my mother's house, and to make it, we worked really hard, sacrificing many things and starving. There were lots of people in the region that came everything turned out very beautiful, except that my brothers and their wives would not speak to me, they saw me and my son with contemp. Like we're stinking, it showed it on their faces hate and indifference. They had parties, constantly, with friends and family, but I was neve invited, my mother and brothers were only go, I wanted to hide from everyone, I felt as if they were ashamed that I was family.

Flower, had problems in her relationship with Sergio, and ended their relationship, so we decided to work together making bricks for ourselves; I took my child and hid him inside the basket bath tub because Eduardo lived very near walking and did not want him to see my baby. He didn't even know that the child was born.

But I got to thinking, that I was doing wrong to hide my son, who cared what people thought of me or my son, I could defend him from all. I kept working, later on my mother. I liked the music and sang occasionally, I took every moment to do what I liked, one time when I was at a party, my mom had caught me she agreed to me being a singer, She took me out the party and started to beat me. She said horrible things to me, that she was ashamed, for I to be an embarsment to her and my family. I force myself to stay quiet, no one knew what had happened and so my mother killed my dream, my dream of being a recognized singer. Ever since I was little I had dreamed of singing. I was working all the time, but one day i got tired of digging the earth, my mind did not accept the situation in which I was, I wanted to change my life something inside me said that I could change if I wanted, and I did want my life to change. Then I held gripped on the peak with force and I shoved it into the soil, wanting desperately to scream that I was going to fight for my dreams. I swore to myself that I would never dig or make bricks. I was not born for that. I would give anything to change my life. The idea of going to the United States appeared in my mind, I went back home with my son in my arms. My mother was very angry that I had returned from work, I changed as fast as I could and left for Cuenca, to call my brother, who was in New York, when I talked to him, I asked him if he could help me, since he was working all the time.

He had a year and in that country. At first he did not believe me but offered to help me, once I was there. He said, looks like, I cannot help you, He told me to find a way to come over here, but in spite of not having his help, I was determined to leave Ecuador place; and nothing could stop me.

Chapter 8

J went back to the house, I had to wait for the car to take me back I was a little sad and disillusioned. I was doubting that my dreams would ever come true, the return was a bit slow, as I walked even saw this guy, who I knew from my brother, Benito was the name of the guy, and in time we had worked with him. He came over and started talking to me, I told him about my brother and my family, he looked at my son and wondered is it yours? I said yes. The guy was very kind to me and my family, so as we talked, we talked about plans to go to America, he knew that my family had needs and knew that my father had died, I look at my baby and said "I Really want to go to America!." He shook his head and agreed to help me, but I want to know who is going to help you go to United States, is a lot of money and I want to know, to whom I will give it to. You know, I could not forgive myself if something bad happened. Accepted it without thinking, and Don Benito walked me to see the coyote, I was going to cross with, he wanted everything to go well and I thanked God I found him that day.

I had to go to apply for my passport, I had an emergency the cross was going to cost $ 6,500,00 it was a lot of money, my mother accompanied me to Cuenca the next day, she was going to take care of my son while I got my passport. My mother was very angry, she wanted to know who would I leave my son with in the way, I wonder? and I said, that I would leave him with my aunt. She was silent and said nothing more. Then I said, would you take care of him for me?! I would greatly appreciate it, if you agree, she did not want me to go, then we had a long talk, I explained my reasons and I think she understood, and ended up helping me out. That weekend I went to Quito but there was a lot of people.

It tore my heart, for having to leave my son, I arrived at the bus terminal with, my mother, my sister Flor, Antonio and his wife and my baby, it was as if half of my life to stay with them after leaving the bus in Quito, I took a plane that would take me to Costa Rica, from there I took another to Guatemala, all that would tour in one day, at the end of the day we met with other people, and planned to stay in a hotel, because a group had just left. We had to wait two weeks to leave for Mexico, but would spend the first by a place called Tecuman; would like as 3:00 am we crossed a river called the Black River, the water came up to my neck, so we to take our clothes off and take it to the head in a plastic bag, it was the only way to cross the river. when we crossed rested the rest of the day, and came out at 1am. to reach other people, unfortunately we could only move at night, and three days after we arrived in Masatenango, was already a town, we were there about a month we could not leave Mexico. There was a lot of vigilance, these days was visiting Pope John Paul ll. were waiting, and at about 4am heard, loud and screaming people, imigration! imigration!!! we all tried to run and flee, but it had us surrounded, we all stopped, we were more than 60 people in total, we were treated like criminals and we just wanted to change our lives and that of our special families. We were taken to D. F. In the capital, i was locked up with other women, for seventeen days. When I left there, I called Rafael, who was in New York. I asked him to help me to buy the flight back to Ecuador. at 2:00 am. We boarded the plane and arrived in Quito, arriving in Ecuador, we also stopped about two hours, i no longer had money to return to Cuenca, thanks to a man who also returned with the passage helped me to come home. It was about eight in the morning, when I arrived my mother almost faints in seeing me back, I did not want to return home. I got some rest, and I left at 5:00 am, I went to get the coyote that was going to to help me cross to the United States, the deal was that we would spend as many times as necessary, I would cross over and I said I was ready to leave immediately, but I had lost my passport, and had to get a new one, as I had no money he gave me a little for the costs, I was in a hurry and rushed, I was stressed. On the way back, I got into an accident just as I was crossing the street, a car hit me, the car was fleeing from the police, it had crossed a red light hit me when i was going through all was dark i knew nothing. and did not know anything.

Chapter 9

I opened my eyesand began to recover I was laying on a bed and realized that I was in a clinic or hospital, I knew by the smell of the place, I really hurt my knee, and when I woke up I saw that I had 24 stitches put in my left knee. I woke up scared, some doctors came and comforted me, for they knew, what had happened to me, but they told me not to worry, for the costs, as they had caught the man who hit me with the car. I was worried thought I could not travel, but that's not going to stop me in my decision, I begged the Dr. to help me, I did not want to lose the only opportunity to go to the U.S., it was risky but he understood me and helped me.

The man who caused the accident, also paid the taxi which took me to the house, my knee hurt a lot, but I holded the pain in, so that my mother would not be frightened; I call the coyote to explain my situation, I told him I was telling good, he told me that it is the only opportunity!, You know if you lose money or not! So my mother and the wife of my brother helped me cure my knee. The rest of the day I rested and the next morning at eight o'clock in the morning, I went out for Quito. Taking my medications and antibiotics, this time I flew to San Salvador, from there to Guatemala. There I had problems with my knee, some friends helped me making me cures. I remove the points from the wound and follow the path, then I travel by car to Mexico. We were hiding; we recrossed the black river, some cameras use gums cars. We went from village to village hidden, so we come to Sinaloa, northern Mexico. We had to wait to cross the desert, about four days, my knee was bothering me again. it hurt a lot and dismissed as a bad smell, it took almost a month to get to Agua Prieta, we finally arrived at the border and stayed in a small cabin. we were with many people and we were very uncomfortable; The situation was very difficult for all, we ate what little they had and sometimes we were left without food, when we ate we would eat just tortilla and fried bean. For me it was all different, but I had to eat even as the road was long and tiring, it was already two weeks and I finally could leave this place, we went at 2.00 am and on the way my knee began to hurt me a lot, when I remove the bandages that covered my wound again note that stink. It scared me, knowing that my knee was rotting; I took all the antibiotics I brought, and put on my wound, also took pain drugs, and had almost no, two people had helped me all the way, and now I think they were my angels, by how selfless help me. We walked about four hours for Piedras Negras, The road was very bad, there were many thorns, it was very dry and many stones on the road, and we met another group of people who were also trying to reach the United States. We were already more than fifty people in total. all came to end Finix Arizona, But there, Immigration arrest us, wanting some ran away, none made it, we were sent back to Mexico. As we reach the same small house where we had been before. Again we were there for days waiting, the four days as smugglers, we climbed in a van, and knocked down a fence and a wall. to enter the other side. We arrived back to back to Arizona. three days, I had to wait, my brother could not send money to continue the journey, I only needed for the flight. we waited, we were locked, sitting and sleeping on the floor, each time waiting to get out. When the smugglers received the money, they took us out of the place and sent us to our final destination. Finally it was my turn and I left directly to New York. In search of my dreams . . .

Chapter 10

I did not know where he was going to show up, all i knew was my brother would find me, but he had to work and sent a friend to pick me up, his friend got lost and did not arrive, there were many people there that would bring their families or friends. One of them asked me if anyone was going to pick me up i said yes my brother but he was not here yet. Then came Immigration officials and asked a group of us for our legal papers I said we had just arrived, they questioned us and took us to a place outside the airport about thirty minutes away, i was very afraid i thought I had to go back again after so much sacrifice, I did not want to return to Ecuador. They took our fingerprints and photographs and then they let us go, among those of us was a man who had been in New York. He had told us that he would take us to a taxi that would take us where we had to go. When we arrived i immediately called my brother on the phone to tell him that I was fine and had already arrived. He told me that his friend was lost and did not arrive at the airport and later on he went to get me, he lived at the time in 106 and 2nd ave in Manhattan. Everything was different, I missed my son and my family i did not know how long I would be here but I was happy to see my brother. I was amazed to see so many buildings, so many cars and people of different races. Rafael shared the apartment with other friends they were all boys. they got drunk a lot, for me it was very uncomfortable, sometimes I slept on the floor and other times in the bed of my brother three of his friends shared a small room with us, but at last I was in New York, three days later i found a friend that was from Sinicay, she already had time in New York she lived in the same building on the first floor and we lived on the sixth floor, she had just found out that I arrived, I went to look for her I was very happy to see her again, I knew I would not be alone, and that she could help me later on.

She invited me to her apartment and we prepared a good meal we were happy to meet again, she was working and told me that she would help me get a job too. Only when she rested, the two of us would go out to buy clothes, I had finally found a job at a laundromat, i ironed shirts and learned to use four machines, i entered at eight in the morning and left at seven in the evening from Monday to Saturday and sometimes Sundays. If i worked on Sundays i earned about $ 400.00 Dollars with what I earned, I started to send money to my mother and my son, i would also send money to Benito to pay him for the money he had lent me. i wanted to give him $ 200.00 Dollars a month, but he wanted me to pay him all together. So I started to save and to limit as much as I could. Three months later, we moved to Queens on 91st. and Roosevelt Rd. my brother would leave to get drunk and more on the weekends. I had to go to work every day from Queens to Manhattan, i still did not know the subway system so I would missed the train many times, arriving late to work. My boss would be angry, I told him what was happening, and he laughed and understood he said it was no problem! that they would pick me up every day to go to work since they lived in Flushing. After that I had no problem coming to work on time.

Chapter 11

One day that i had gone to work I thought I have seen from the distance Rosendo, my ex-boyfriend, the son of Mrs. Bernarda. But I thought it was impossible, there were many people in this great city, but then I thought, my brother on occasions got together with him to drink. One day that i was off from work, someone knocked on the door i was not expecting anyone, I went out to see who it was I was surprised to see Rosendo in front of the door i did not know what to say, I froze, through my mind rushed a lot of memories like a film in a movie, i invited him in and build up courage to ask why did you leave me? Why did play with my heart? Why did you leave like that? Why didn't you call or write to me? I paused, then i had to tell him about the relationship I have had with his friend Eduardo and that I had a son that I had left with my mother in Ecuador. I also told him what Eduardo told me about Rosendo hating me and never wanting to see me again. I yelled you're a bastard! I did not deserve this! I loved you with all my heart i was in rage. i was so full of anger, cursed him and told him everything that i could think of. He denied everything and asked me if i received the letter? i asked what letter!? he said I sent a letter when i had just arrived in New York for you, i quickly told him i did not receive it. We both cried together and we agreed we had many things to clarify we started to talk about everything that had happened, and he said i still love you and that he never had forgotten about me and asked me to give him a chance and that time would clarify many things. Seeing him again, I realized that I still loved him, I told him that would give him another try, he worked in a building and I still worked at the cleaners. We would get together sometimes and go out and sometimes he would take me to work. He taught me how to ride the train so I would not get lost, he started to go more occasionally to my house, and sometimes would bump into my brother Rafael but on the weekends they would drink a lot and i did not like that. I thought that would change, I was more in a hurry to raise money so i can pay back Mr. Benito, I would save as much money as possible, so I got up at 4am to make my lunch so i won't have to spend it outside. I would just spend money on my subway fair. After a while i saved up on a lot of money that i thought was too much, so I made a hole in the mattress where I slept and attached $ 5,000.00 Dollars. I quickly send the money to Ecuador to pay the debt that i had with Mr. Benito but also i send some money to my mother. After a while Rafael started to notice that me a Rosendo had a relationship but he did not like that, he would get drunk and insulted me, and hit me I was slapped and kicked he was not caring that I was his sister. He yelled "You did not come here to have a boyfriend, you came here to work for your son", I kept quiet and just took the hits he would give me. When i talked on the phone with my mother she would ask me how was i doing and i would always say i was okay although it was not true. But since my mom knew her children and knew that something was wrong, others have already told her that my brother would beat me when he got drunk, she knew the suffering that i had to go through because of my brother.

One Sunday I called my family in Ecuador, my brother Antonio told me he wanted to come to America. I told Antonio, now I cannot help you because as you know I just paid the money i owed to Mr. Benito I told him if he would wait I would be glad to help him. He talk to my brother Raphael for a long time, I guess Antonio decided to come to the United States either way. He went to Guatemala and then Mexico and in three weeks he was here i was so happy to have my other brother with me.

Chapter 12

When Antonio arrived, we went to buy him some clothes and a bed to sleep in. It took him a week to find a job; his first job was as an assistant in construction. I felt calmer because Antonio and I had a good relationship between brother and sister, we shared many things. He told me that the reason he had come was to take care of me, that our mother had told him how bad Rafael treated me and from now on he was going to protect me. At first everything was going great. But Rafael would get drunk and had friends over. Antonio had asked him not to drink at home, and if you want to drink, do it elsewhere. Have respect for us! he yelled. But no case to the contrary, he was intoxicated and was more aggressive with me, he came to beat, he humiliated me in front of his friends, and asked me to respect him for being the older brother.

Antonio and I wanted to move, but we did not want to leave him alone, if not for that he got drunk and humiliated us, no problem. I did not want to leave, as he had helped to reach the United States. Sometimes when we worked and Rafael was drunk, and we hung out on a walk and sometimes I would arrive late to avoid being hit and assaulted by him. Rafael hit me all the time, for no reason, and when one day he saw . . .

A day that Antonio saw what was gonig on he told him that he and my mother knew. How he treated me, they argued and ended up angry, but we still lived together, the following weekend, he got drunk again, so me and Antonio, we had to stay in a small room while Rafael drunk all night, the next day, we went to work tired from not sleeping well; I came back from work like arround 5.00pm, as soon as I entered the apartment, I saw that Rafael was still getting drunk, and without knowing why, he began kicking me, I just covered my face, he gave me a lot of kicks and punches. I felt pain everywhere, and I thought he was going to kill me. Thanks to a friend of his, he stopped, hitting me. His friend asked, why? Why do you hit your sister?, I yelled and I asked him why did he hit me, what did I do? And I wondered, he asked who's that guy, with whom were you, and who were you on the beach?

I was surprised, I was working and even though I denied it, they did not believe me, according to that someone had said, they saw me on the beach with a man, walking calmly. But I did not want to argue, I went to the street all beaten; I wanted to call Antonio, who had gone to visit a friend in Woodside, it was about twenty minutes from the train stop, when he answered, he heard crying and Rafael told him what I did, not long in coming, he encountered the purple face and bleeding from the blows. He came up to the building, and I followed slowly, because I had the body aches; Rosendo arrived at that time and was very angry when he saw me beaten up. The trouble was coming, because when Antonio entered the apartment he went against Rafael. And asked for an explanation about what he had done to me, he yelled as he hit and punched and told Rafael, She's your sister, not your wife you need to respect her, and continued fightingt, they were very agressive, so we had to get them away and from each other. I thought they were going to kill each other, I really panicked, but Rosendo pulled

Antonio away and I went home after them, Rosendo offered to drive to wherever we wanted, we had to go, it was very late and I was tired, Rosendo took us to a restaurant in Roosevelt av. and 82 st. Since Antonio was very angry, he drank some beers with Rosendo, also ate something and went back to the apartment a little after one in the morning. Rafael was already asleep, so we went without any problems, but if a little scary, the next day, I got up early and made lunch to take to work, for Antonio and me. The two went to work forgetting what had happened, I did not go to work, but Rosendo was waiting at the entrance of the train. He did not know I was not at work, looking for me a little later, we stated talking about what had happen, and he said he doesn't want Rafael hurting me, and suggested me to go and live with him? I did not expect this, but I thought I had problems with my brother. At some point we will move in together!! He say you know I love you and that my greatest desire is to be with you, didn't think much and accepted, as I did not like now I was living with my brother Rafael, I did not deserve that, we went in search of a room; for both of us to live away from my brothers got a room and return later for the little I had, but I had to wait until Rafael was not in the apartment, I did not want to see him because it hurt that he would hurt me, so after I was out of there, Rosendo called his father and told him that he would not go home, not to worry, they lived together, but since then Rosendo would live with me. Rosendo went to work on the third day, he worked with his father at that moment he to his father Mr. Rodolfo that he was living with me and from that moment on we were a couple, even without getting married, I did not know if it was love, but at the moment it was an opportunity to change my life. I wanted to succeed from nothing, just hoped and prayed to God, that i did not do wrong in that decision.

Chapter 13

Rosendo, and his father worked together, after a few days, Rosendo took me out with Mr Rodolfo, and me and Mr Rodolfo started to get along with each other. I was very happy, we went out for a walk and we had fun, we were an amazing family, But it was only about seven months after we moved to another site with my friend Laura and her husband Isidro, we would share the basement apartment that was by the 105 St. By then I did not see my brothers and stop working at the cleaners, I was out of work a few months, but my friend Laura helped me to get one, was at the factory where she worked, she was the same person that I met in my arrival. I got the job, and there I made buttonholes in clothing that was made there. I was paid by the piece. all day came and went from Queens to Manhathan. Laura already had a baby and was expecting another baby, I was pregnant too, and I felt the symptoms, but had not said anything to Rosendo. Laura was fired because of her pregnancy, but I kept working, but as my boos began to notice I was pregnant, I was fired Also, the two us were out of work, we tried to look for jobs, but no one gave us a chance, because our conditions. We were desperate, and began to gather in the trash for cans in the garbage, every day we did the same, that was the only way to get some money, we also got an extra job, we were doing fantasia, wich was assembling jewelry at night and during the day we recycled. first Laura gave birth to their baby. After some more time, I gave birth to a beautiful baby, it was the most beautiful baby and beautiful. I was very happy, I named her Fernanda; Rosendo continued working in the building and I was still in the trash cans recycling. Rosendo would get drunk, but it was not constant, but ever since Fernanda was born, he started to get drunk more often, and to my bad luck, in those days, the mother came from Ecuador, to stay. Since she had arrived, Rosendo went every day to see her, it was every day, they lived in the 93 St.

When I felt better, I found a job, it was in the 42 st Manhathan. in a factory, cleaning and cutting into yarns, not used to the cold New York it was very cold to me. but I used to, we had to work, so is life in any city, Rosendo took days of work, sometimes did not work and went to see his mom. I left my Fernanda, with my friend Laura, a day that Rosendo not work, he offered to care for Fernanda, I accepted and went out to work as I always did. But when I returned, I did not see them in the house, I looked at my friend Laura and ask for them I started to worry me and she told me to calm down. She saw them leave the house at about four in the afternoon, they are good, and they will return, do not worry! she told me. I did not know if she was warm, I was afraid that my baby would get sick. They arrive late at night and I claimed, didn't know where they had been. I was surprised by his reaction, he was angry and yelling, he said, do you want to know? I just wanted to show my baby, and I cry, take my daughter to my mother's house, I want you to Know. There is a problem!

Since then, I noticed many changes in his mood, his attitude was not the same, almost was not in the house, he was always going to his mother's house, it was so bad that when he came home, I was offended, he was rude, and hit me, made me feel as if I was in his way, was an intolerable situation, but kept working. I remembered my mother and call her to tell her what was happening to me. waiting for her tip, but it was the best, she also offended me, she screamed and said things that hurt me, like husband you wanted! now, So, you tell me now! I do not care! that's not my problem! When I listen to mourn. I said, what you are going through. quiet, you have to put up, that's your men.

My mother already knew that Mrs. Bernarda, had come to the United States, for the purpose of separating Rosendo and me. Dona Bernarda, had told some friends of the family would not rest, until you do. She already had a woman that if it suited his son Rosendo, according to her already committed since before Rosendo came to America. Fernanda was about to turn five months since she was born. Rosendo and my friend Laura's husband, Isidro, came to get drunk together, I thought it strange. since they did not celebrate together, returned very late and well drunks. She was restless and had a premonition; Rosendo scared that struck me, as he had done many times and every time I was going to see his mother Laura was the same way, every time Isidro, got drunk; Both were afraid, and they had left a little angry with us. We closed the doors before they arrived, but we could not sleep peacefully, we were unaware that would happen. Was about three in the morning, when they arrived, they made enough noise, and spoke hard. Wanting could not enter, the door was locked and that really upset them. Isidro turned and look for one of the windows and strong kick uan it opened. You could not do anything, they were already inside. we started hitting, kicking, punching and bleeding and very painful end, stopped to see us on the floor. The next day I could not go to work because of the bumps and marks on the face. Rosendo back the next day and it only apologized, he was very sorry and wanted to forgive him, he was drunk, I said! I do not remember what happened to me, sorry, sorry. I swear it does not happen again. I gave him another chance, but I was like two weeks, unable to work, was very lastimada. Me dolia one eye, who closed with a punch, then find another job, I had dismissed the former, Laura and Isidro, not reconciled, so just going to live for a while, what was left of the rest of the month and they were separating. Isidro notice, Rosendo that were, that would leave the apartment, and how, we could not pay all the rent it. also we were moving, I did not want, but there was no way to stay in place, try to find a place, only three of us, but could not find, had but did not accept babies; Desperate Rosendo, went and talked to their parents they accepted, I seemed, did not accept, but nothing could be done, Rosendo was my husband and we had to be together, through thick and thin. We were a family was going through a rough time, like what any other. I thought things would change and that would improve our situation, I was wrong, I never imagined, what was going to happen,

Chapter 14

The hell started for me, because i only got a small space in the room of the house I had to hang some curtains to have a little bit of privacy. We shared some spaces, including the cusine and bathroom, we would prepare our food, I began to seek work in a factory in Manhathan, Rosendo asked his mother to care for Fernanda, I knew she would agree only because it was for his son, he knew I did not like her, and I knew she only did with intentions of seperating me and her son. She changed her attitude when he was here she was very kind and gentle, but when Rosendo left she changed and took every moment to insult me and make me look ridiculous.

We had many fights because of her she made him doubt me, He was no longer the same, he controlled for the time that i was to come home, and if it came a little late, I sure and occasionally hit by the train that delayed me, but he did not care. Mrs. Bernarda, to food for snack early and often fed him his son. So when I bequeathed to and eating, the Lord, and was not hungry and accused me of not attending, compared me to her mother.

Like me no longer ate, ate alone, but sometimes by the courage and rage, I went to bed without trying anything, our relationship was very wrong, but tried to come early and take care of, well, to no avail; Rosendo's mother brought him food in secret from me until the little room we could not stand his indifference and harassment of Mrs., brother had separated from his wife, who was aunt of Rosendo. They had argued for some time, and had not been on good terms. Rafael lied, Rosendo to fight, the party was the most fun. Music fills the air, dancing Rosend and I were in the midst of the guests began to attack me Rosendo and offend. I wanted my brother to leave the place, first he did quietly and suddenly in a violent pump. The gave me a hard slap. Everyone turned to me and I felt very bad, very humiliated. Bothered me a lot and one day no more support. I confronted Mrs.

Bernarda, why, always makes me look bad to his son, who is against me? That gets into my life. ELA ignored me and then told Rosendo. I was tired of everything. Fernanda had almost a year, we were celebrating the christening, everything was ready, but the day of the party, my brother came in search of me, saying that I had invited him. Rafael and Rosendo were upset because my brother had ended their relationship with the aunt of Rosendo. Rosendo was dancing with me and quietly claim the presence of my brother, I told him that I had not invited, but, did not believe me. The music fills the air, and in a fit of rage, Rosendo, began assaulting and yelling in front of the guests. He gave me a sharp slap in front of people and humiliate me, Mrs. Bernarda seemed to enjoy everything came and took my arm, and I said, we are a while for you to hide, while you miss the courage; hide for a while, avoid more problems, took me to his room and left me there, but put out cerradura. Me key to leave locked in my daughter's party, was to open the door after two in the morning; I only went to use the bathroom. When the party's over, I felt very bad, know, that was a victim of domestic violence. It made me normal, every couple pence would have problems following day rose about eleven o'clock in the morning, and all claims, which I did. and my daughter Fernanda, I hid those hours and still had not seen and did not know how it was. This time, I went back to listen to excuses ever. Excuse me, not that I spend! I do not remember! sure, your brother caused me! You know you can not stand and do not like. It seems that the mom was listening, that appeared immediately, and again began to criticize and get into my life. Rosendo, ignored me and went to take a bath, was still not out when they arrived, the godfathers of Fernanda, wanted to continue the party, were very happy to sponsor Fernanda, They asked me, because I had gone to the party, I had to lie and say that I felt very bad, I apologize for what happened. After that day, we agreed on how we would divide up the duties, we wanted to build our house in Ecuador and we would divide the costs, I played payable, income and expenses of the house, and what was won Rosendo to build our house. There were many expenses for rent, food, and other, so I had to find another job, packing costume jewelry in the evenings at home. From what I earned, paid, income, pampers, food, my travel and also Mrs Bernarda, by taking care of Fernanda. Work hard, but I did not care, I wanted to have my own house and also, to move from there, barely slept two or three hours and then I vat to another job, it seemed that everything was going well, Rosendo, sent money to build the house, take care not to Sali pregnant again, but Rosendo did not know it. He found out one day that I got sick and I had gone to the hospital, I was not expecting, when alerted to the not care, I just said ahhhh, another baby, or modo. lo only good thing is that I was working well, that weekend he asked me, how are you? well, I said. just stayed silent, I went to make dinner. I call for us to eat and told me to wait, their parents eat with us, he said he wanted to send a TV to Ecuador, but I stranger whom? He said that for the aunt, only said, okay.

The parents arrived and went immediately to send the damn TV. Back to the house, they found a cousin and his wife. they came together to the house, going to bring two six pac of beer, after dinner, began to get drunk, and talked and talked, but I heard something, that I care, cousin, I asked Rosendo. How is she? Already control the TV or not?. Rosendo and beckoned him to shut up, I remain doubtful, the cousin's wife also was drinking, approached me and said something that upset me a lot. ! Lend me your husband and I lend mine! Angry I said, if you want to give it to you, take it, and kept talking, not caring that the husband was not respected presente. Ella or very foolish. Rosendo. The next day I apologized for everything that happened. I told him about his cousin's wife and gave laughter! If I want, I can go with it, and that! stops also claim me, you always do.

No matter what you do and do not do. just go and silent, since then I knew that this relationship was going to end, I thought of my children, I keep quiet and hold me, another humiliation.

Chapter 15

Rosendo, had two jobs he was the superintendent of a building in Brooklyn and one in 72 st. in Queens. My pregnancy kept advancing and soon after i could not work anymore. So I went to see the lady who gave me the job to assemble the costume jewelry from there I would work in the house and I did not have to pay Mrs. Bernarda for taking care of Fernanda. One night i had heard Rosendo talk on the phone with a woman, i was really surprised to hear him speak so familiarly with the women. He was speaking to her about a TV and also about a withdraw $ 2,000.00 dollars he had sent. After a few days, I felt a little bad and left for the hospital i had gone to Manhattan at Mount Saint

Hospital. I went alone, i took some pampers and some clothes for the baby, Rosendo had gone to work and could not accompany me, according to him he would go in the evening to check up on me. It got darker and he did not show up, hours passed and i was going into labor i had giving birth to a beautiful boy. The next day at six in the morning I called to asked why didn't he show up, he answered and came out with the excuse that he had a lot of work that when he had arrived home he was very tired, He just asked me when was coming out the hospital i said later on in the afternoon he replied to me and said to take a cab home and that his mother would pay before the end of the call, i asked him what were we going to name the baby he said with non importance Oswaldo I agreed and asked him for second name he said annoyed name him whatever i wanted that it was my choice. In my country it is custom to put two names for the babies, I named him Oswaldo and he had my last name not his father's last name like Fernanda. I took a cab home and asked the driver to wait for me to get money as i was entering the house Ms. Bernarda came out holding Fernandas hand to pay for the cab. I went to accommodate the baby in my bed, I was a little tired and wanted to rest a bit, before I asked for Rosendo his mother apologized for him and said my son is working and that's why he could not have gone to see me in the hospital. The only glad one of my arrival and the baby was my Fernanda, Rosendo arrived about eleven o'clock at night. He laid over the bed and took Fernanda and hugged her against him, and with a mocking voice said "you see Fernanda we have another cry baby in our house" referring it to the baby. and still teasing me he looked at me and he laughed, His mother called us telling us to come and eat, after eating Rosendo held Oswaldo for a small second and then put him down a went to rest We were like two strangers, the next day, I woke up and he was almost about to leave to work and asked me what i was going to do today I said I will do laundry and pay the rent for this month he asked me do you have money? I nodded yes I went to wash and get on with my routine. I started looking for a job again; my motives were my two children. My boss that helped me by recommended me to someone else; I had a little more money because of sticking beads and ornaments. Rosendo hardly spoke to me, he would come home from work and go with his parents, they used to talk to him in secret and I was curious I felt uncomfortable, I had the feeling that something bad was going to happen, They chatted and made sure i wouldn't listen. That was enough for me to think that it was something wrong and that they were plotting something evil against me, i returned back to the room immediately and Rosendo followed me i asked him "what secrets do you and your mother have" and he yelled "that's none of your business I keep quiet and said, someday I'll know and I hope it's nothing bad, our relationship remained the same it was hell for me since they ignored me and acted like if I did not exist. Rosendo kept sending money to Ecuador for the purpose of the "construction of our home," I was still paying the costs and seeking the welfare of my children. Finally one day he said, "the house is finished!" now you just have to save a little more, I thought my expenses would reduce and Rosendo would help me, but i was wrong, he started to get drunk with his cousin and the cousin's wife more often, I was tired of that situation and decided that i was gonna work to fix my teeth and i was not gonna pay for the rent anymore, wanted to fix my teeth that i had lost on one occasion when he punched me, he was not fond of me wanting to fix my teeth he would make fun of me and call me names. Oswaldo was only two months of age and one night Rosendo had come home very drunk so drunk he could not get out the car i could hear clearly because the parking lot was right behind the house. I heard his parents race down to help him and Rosendo spoke very loud and his mother telling him to shut up. I could hear very clearly everything he was saying he told his mother "i talked to her and she told me she

finished the house, mom I'm soon gonna be with her"
his mom told him to be quiet i asked myself Who was
she? i asked myself was he gonna leave with another
women i have heard before him talk to a girl named
Camila and that he had already sent $ 1,500.00 Dollar
i listened to many things that hurt me and that i did
not want to remember, I could not sleep, the next day
he was going to hang out with some buddies at the
beach. I did not know, I found out when his mother
asked him if he was ready. I asked him what had
happened the night before, who was Camilla? He
denied everything and said he did not remember, so I
went and asked Mrs. Bernarda, I said I know
everything and she just smiled and said, yes! it is true,
he will go with Camila, that I came to separate you
from him and that he was already engaged ever since
he came from Ecuador, I said, what about the
children? don't you feel sorry for then there your
grandchildren but she did not care, she was upset and
wanted to beat me, but I stopped her and told her
"don't you dare you will never lay another finger on
me", I was very angry and said the truth hurts but she
should not get involved that the problems the me and
Rosendo had was only between me and him. She
started to tease me, Rosendo came from behind and
started beating me Bernarda got in and took me from
the hair, I tried to let go, but she grabbed on harder by

my hair and pulled a lot of my hair, i could see my hair in the woman's hand. i cried helplessly and said why would a man that loved me so much treat me like that. I could see the woman smile with my hair between his fingers; Some neighbors came to rescue me because they knew how they treated me. Thanks to them, they stopped beating me I distanced myself from them and went to cook for the children because Rosendo was going to eat with his mother, and took Fernanda, i would eat by myself. Everything was hell, Oswaldo had already turned four months, since it was a weekend and he said when he came back from work that we would go all out together to get the kids ready that he would just take out the trash from the Brooklyn building and return. He said he wanted to take us to McDonalds I said okay then I will buy some pampers for the baby, but he offered to go, I gave him $ 20.00 Dollars to buy them, not wanting to fight and stayed silent, As time went by he did not return, I thought he had gone to Brooklyn and had found his friends, the children and i kept waiting, it was night still no sign of him i decided to call him but he did not respond, the next day came Don Rodolfo came in and asked where was Rosendo and if he had arrived? I told him I he had not arrived. I suspect something, but did not say anything and left for work I went up to the old Bernarda and I asked her to look after

Oswaldo for a while because i could only take Fernanda. I went to Brooklyn where Rosendo worked but found out that he didn't even take out the trash I started to worry, I went to the hospital to precincts i looked in Queens, the Bronx, i asked Ms. Bernarda if she knows anything about her son she just told me that he will appear soon enough. The afternoon came and Rodolfo came back i wanted to go and look for him again but Mrs. Rudolph Bernarda and would not let me, they went for me. But when they left I went out to look for a man who lived in the apartment and asked him to call to Ecuador and ask his aunt if she had seen Rosendo because his aunt lived right next to the house of Rodolfo. She replied that Rosendo had arrived to Ecuador since Monday. The news surprised me so much and i thought their parents knew and did not tell me. Bernarda came and wonder if her son had arrived and I said no. On Tuesday I waited Bernarda to leave so i can go out with my kids. I had nowhere to go but I did not care, I wanted to leave as far as possible from the and from the hell i lived in, i called a friend of mine and asked her to help me I told her about my situation she agreed to help me. I started to pack my things and of my children, i only packed some clothes for my children and a few clothes for me. When I finished i took a taxi and went to my friend's house. It was the third day I left The House of

Bernarda, and I learned, that day rosendo and camilla were getting married. I live in the 94st with my friend and then started looking for work because I was left with nothing, went back to look for my friend Laura she worked selling ice cream, she got me working again. I wanted to find a room for my kids and I. I was determined to do anything for my children.

Chapter 16

I used to sell ice cream but still did not have enough money. Then I started looking for another job bagging jewelry fantasies. A month later I gather some money and started to search for a room to rent but the majority did not want to give me a room because of my children. I found a lady and she offered me her house and gave me a little place in her living room we only had a mattress bed that the lady had gave us. Our clothes were in trash bags and we did not have a place to cook, my kids and I ate bread with malt. When I would go to work I left my children with a lady so she may take care of them it kept me calm to know that at least my kids ate better. Sometimes my children misbehaved and behaved badly and call her Mrs. Attention. One day Oswaldo asked the lady for some cereal and she gave him but that was not the kind of cereal he wanted he had wanted the same thing Fernanda ate so he started crying, so the lady climbed Oswaldo into the tub and bathed him with ice cold water. She thought it would be a good for him so he won't do it again, I didn't know anything until later on. My mother did not know anything about Rosendo leaving me. She found out by other people and she was very angry she took some pictures of the kids that I had sent to her and brought it to the parish priest back in Ecuador. My mother wanted to force Rosendo to recognize my children as his own, the priest did what he could, but he only recognized fernanda. Rosendo denied having lived with me and denied being the father of my son Oswaldo. My brother Rafael, visited me and advised me that I would be better off going back to Ecuador he said "return to Ecuador go over there! Who will help you with the kids here?" I thought my brother would support me and motivate me to get ahead, but it was not happening, he was so negative towards me but I did not lose faith, I continued selling ice cream, I wanted to raise money, so me and my children can eat well, I wanted to fix my teeth and baptize my son Oswaldo, I continued to live in that little room in very poor condition and with extreme needs, our breakfast and dinner was only malt and bread, that was what I was feeding my children. A couple of days ago I had met a guy named martin he was the nephew of Don Guillermo and we had seen each other on several occasions but did not talk. One day I came home from work, I went out with the kids and he found us and invited us to go eat somewhere, I was surprised when he had said he was looking for me and that he knew of my problem and wanted to help me, I did not believe him, but I saw my children and thought of their needs. I went to lunch with him and we started to try to know each other better, he often sought and offered me his help, we spent about two months and one Sunday I went to hear Mass, it was a little cloudy I was thinking if I should give him a chance and if I would be doing the right choice. I was desperate of seeing my children suffer and eating only bread and drinking malt, it made me take the decision to accept his proposal, I said that the only reason I accepted is for my children. He agreed and told me, I'll never regret having accepted to live with him. We looked for an apartment that day and found one in 103 Street, we moved a week later it was a Wednesday, I remember because I promised myself that day, that everything would change for me and my children.

Chapter 17

When I started to live with Martin I really thought my life would change, he worked in construction and I worked in selling ice cream. Everything looked amazing I saw him as a sweet man he was very kind to my other children and liked carrying Oswaldo. I was happy, because although he was not the father he was very affectionate with my two children that were not even his. I went to work eager to get ahead in life, there was no more nightmares in my life. After one year, he began to change I had gotten pregnant, but he did not like the idea he did not want me to have the baby, and one day he came home drunk and started beating me for no reason. He had been driving a van, and had called me to go and pick him up because he felt very drunk. I decided not to go because it was too late and I had no one to leave my children with, so when he got home he started to hit me and gave me kicks and punches. Already on the floor I covered my stomach because I did not want to lose my baby. But it was hopeless I started bleeding a lot and lost my baby of two months. I cried immensely at the loss of my baby and also because from that day he started to get drunk more often and started to beat me more and offended me and after all of that he would always come back and apologize for hurting me and always promised me it won't happen again. I was stupid enough to believe him. So we lived together over two years, and then I got pregnant again, he would still hit me and the neighbors from the first floor always helped me several times, until one day he hit me savagely and my children had asked for help through the phone , the neighbors had called the emergency number and the cops came. My kids were scared; it was always the same thing over and over   was allowing my children to get traumatized by the violence that was going on in my home. After that day a few people came to my home and identified themselves as social workers from the city of New York, they asked me some questions about how and why was martin treating me so bad, I was very afraid and denied everything, but they also wanted to talk to the kids, I could not refuse they took them to the small room and talked with them they asked them many questions. I did not know what they had said and when they finished talking to the kids they left, knowing that it was true on how martin would beat me.

The next day they came again, but this time they showed up with two cops I was very scared, but especially when one of them told me that they were gonna take the children with them. I was terrified and scared that they were gonna my beloved children away from me that I fainted. I did not know what to do I just cried, they had to take me to the hospital and when I woke up I immediately looked for my children but they were nowhere, a social worker came and explained what had happened and she told me that for the moment I could not see the children and that I had an appointment for the next day I had to go to court, the judge told me that the kids could not go on living in those conditions and with those problems and that i had to decide whether I wanted to have my children back or stay with martin? Martin had accompanied me to court that day, there the judge told me that they was going to investigate me, since someone had called the city because I mistreated the children. He said the children are at high risk in that situation and that I was allowed to see my children only on Wednesday until the investigations finished, I could not do anything, so I accepted to go see them on the days they let me. When i would go see my children I would cry but at the same time I was happy and thankful for god allowing me to see them, I would give them a big hug and told them to forgive me for allowing this to happen and to not worry because this was gonna be over very soon that it was just a matter of time. They only gave me thirty minutes to see my children, after visiting my children that day one of the social workers told me that I had an appointment in court the next day with the judge. The next day I was really scared, did not know what was going to happen; I prayed a lot and asked God to help me. I think God helped me and the judge notified me that they would return me my children but with the condition that Martin was out of the house or I find another place to go and live with children. Martin was put a restraining order and could not get close to children or me. Later on that day I told Martin to put himself in my place, what would he do? He made the decision to leave. The judge sent him a letter saying that he was not allowed near us. I was sent to take therapy and family counseling classes, they said that my children would return back home with me on Friday at 5.00 pm. I was sent to Jamaica Queens to sign some papers and arranging for therapy, the next day I left early to pick up my children from the shelter, I was sent to another place in Manhattan near a river I didn't know how to get there but I kept on asking people until I reached the site. I finally got my kids I was the happiest women in this world at the moment and also because I was pregnant again. I asked a lady to take care of children while I worked; Missing a month to give birth, I was told that my rent was going to be raised, I started to worry because with what I earned was not enough. Where I worked, I had been working with relatives of Martin, and they knowledge of my problem and they offered to help. They invited me to share their apartment near the 107 Vivian Street and North End Boulevard. I started to feel sick and went to hospital in Manhattan, there I gave birth to a precious little girl, again alone, with no one to help me return to apartment and immediately went out to the market to buy food for the children, I could not rest; My children depended on me alone. The next week I had to revise the baby in the hospital. I named her Natalia, I went to the appointment and back pass by the other children. For a while my life was normal, I kept working and tried the best for children, some time went by and one day i was surprised to see Martin approach to talk to me, he said he wanted to help with the cost of the baby's drinks. He already knew that the money was not enough and also said that he was sorry, he loved me and he wanted to get back with me he wanted to have a family with me. I had my doubts because in the time I lived with him I had many problems, I lost a baby and almost lost Natalia, I remembered the day when he came home and threw 200.00 dollars at me and told me to get rid of the baby that I wasn't ready and to get an abortion, it all came back to me like a flashback, only that to him it seemed forgotten. The next day I had an appointment to take Natalia to the hospital and coming back at two in the afternoon, I stopped by the daycare to pick Oswaldo up, just as I was going in I was sent to the office, there I was told that my child had been taken by two social workers from the city, and they had left a letter for me also telling me that I had to give my other children in. The social worker from the daycare told me that it would be better that I do as they say, it hurt my heart that I had to give up my children again but what broke my heart completely was that I had to give up Natalia she was just 5 days old. I felt like my world ended, I had to go to Jamaica Queens, when I arrived the social workers were already waiting for me, I asked them if Oswaldo was okay and they said he was fine, I begged them to help me, I did not want my children to be taken away from me again.

They just said they were gonna start to investigate on what has happened! The next day they came to the house to see in what conditions we were living, they told me, I had to have a crib and clothes for the baby. For not having that they took my children away from me for 3 weeks until I had what was necessary, those 3 weeks to me where lasting forever but they returned them to me. I kept on going to therapies and counseling which helped me a lot, I didn't want to lose my children again, so I started to sell tamales with another lady, she would cook them and I would go out and sell it. I left my children with a lady that would take care of them while I would go out and work. I had to be a little cautious while working because I could not get caught by the police, but one day I got caught and the police arrested me for 24 hours no matter how much I told them to let me go for my children they didn't listen to me I was devastated to what my children were thinking what had happened to me and why didn't I come home after I was let free i ran to go pick up my children. Three days later I went back to selling ice cream now, I wanted to give my children the best and I did not need no man to do so, A month later the police caught me again and arrested me for selling ice cream I was locked up for 12 hours, after that had happened I decided to go sell ice cream in Brooklyn, Natalia was

turning eight months when Martin started to look
for us he wanted to see his daughter, he knew he had
the restraining order but did not care. He begged me
to let him see the child that he had come all the way
from New Jersey, I did not want to deny him from
seeing his daughter he was the father, I thought of the
pain that I went through when social services took my
children. He started coming more often to see Natalia,
on some occasions he did not want to leave so he
stayed over. And I would do the same routine I would
normally do, I would take Oswaldo to daycare and
drop off Fernanda in school and then drop off Natalia
with her babysitter. But one day it was cloudy and
my boss returned me from work because we couldn't
work in those conditions so my plan was to go pick up
something really quick from home and then pick up
my children and spend the rest of my day with them,
but as I approached home I saw Martins car parked
outside I thought maybe he had not gone to work. As
I entered the apartment I was shocked to see Martin
and his so called "cousin" having intimate relations
in my bed, I could not believe what I was seeing, I
could not stand it and went against women but I was
reaching to hit the women I was stopped by martin he
pulled me back and started to hit me while his cousin
got away I quickly slipped his hits and went after her
but then again Martin grabbed me and started to hit

me again, when he saw I was lying on the floor on continuons he left like nothing and left me lying there, when I started to regain continuons I went to go pick up my kids I went to pick up the kids and returned home I started to cook and fed my children, I was so hurt I could not be calm because of what happened I was disappointed I was so full of emotions but I hid it because I did not want my kids to see like that. Martin returned home at about five in the afternoon, but he went straight to his cousins room I could hear them talking and after awhile he came out and approached me and started insulting me and was extremely mad at the fact that I was trying to hit his cousin, we started arguing and he grabbed my hair and pulled it down then he kicked me in my stomach and as I bend over because of the kick he punched me in my face and broke my nose. He did not care one bit as I begged him to stop and not hit me no more, he still kept on hitting me he picked me up and ripped my shirt off, I was covered in blood as he hit me I quickly heard one of his cousin's voice telling him to stop and then pulled him away. I quickly told my children to hand me the phone and dialed the police I was in high pain I felt like if any minute I was gonna faint and my children were scared. When police arrived, they asked me if I was okay, I looked terrible and one of the cops told me ma'am you have a serious problem you need to choose whether your children or him without a doubt in my mind said my children, they were the most important thing in this world to me. The police arrested Martin for domestic violence, after that I stayed scared and was afraid because as the police was putting martin in the car Martin yelled and said that we came out he was gonna kill me, but the police told me not to be afraid that the more he kept threatening me the more charges will go against him, after they\ left I went to see my children they too were scared I locked myself in the room with them, they only had me now.

Chapter 18

I started to receive help from the city and they also agreed to help me with housing, but I had to go to a shelter in Brooklyn, with so many problems I completely forgot about my son Joseph, who was in Ecuador with my mother, I could not send money or had called him, I only trusted my mother to look after him. Some of my sisters did not like my son Jose and took every chance to bother him and to put him against me they would say things such as your mother doesn't love you that's why she never calls and I would never find out. I was concerned on what might happen to my children, I decided to go to a shelter. When I got there they asked me so many questions but they were very kind to me and my children, they gave us a room for me and my children with a bunk bed and a crib for my baby, they also gave us clothes and food and other things we needed, our life took a complete change. I felt strange there were so many people of different races and colors, speaking different languages. We would all gather for breakfast in the basement and we would also share the bathroom, on some occasions we would have to wait on line to use the bathroom. It was very difficult for me at first and made me the question of whether it was worth coming here with my children. But what else could I do? They had me only, many times we did not have a place to sit down and eat so we would have to eat standing up. Watching my children eat made tears roll down my eyes they were so innocent and did not know of our circumstances, as the tears rolled down my eye I would quickly suck them back in I did not want them to see me cry I wanted to be strong for my children. My children were a little bit active because we couldn't go out a lot so they would run around the building and often other kids would bully and bother them I was troubled by this, I spoke to one of the social workers there her name was Priscilla, I told her I felt intimidated in that place as some of the other women that had been there longer bothered me. I felt powerless again for not changing the situation in which I and my children were living in. She listened and asked me to be patient, I was desperate I wanted my life to change once and for all. Priscila told me to hold out a little longer and to ignore the people who bothered me, for my children she told me to think about their future and that this nightmare will end soon. She helped me to go to family counseling classes and receive therapies for domestic violence; i took advantage those classes because they were when my children were in school. My children would go to school right near the shelter we were living in so i would drop them off every day and head to therapies; I took therapies three times a week. I would never get tired of praying to god to help us so the lives of me and my children would change.

The wait was an eternity to me, it was stressful to be in the shelter, watching the same people every day and with the same problems and nothing seemed to change; Priscila only gave me encouragement, but one day she arrived with an application for an apartment I doubted what she was saying as I was losing faith I would keep all the bagged food that they gave us, Priscilla had told me that when I moved to an apartment I could take all the bags. One day I took my children to school so I was left only with Natalia when I came back I heard my name called by the speaker; immediately I went down to see what happened. Priscilla was waiting for me and said "Esperanza take this card, this card will change you and your children's life you can now buy food for the kids and for you and the same amount will be added every month, as she told me this tears rushed down my eyes, I was very grateful I gave thanks to Priscilla and to all the workers there and gave them a hug and then I said thank you god for blessing·me and my children. Then she told me Esperanza you and your kids are almost set to move into your new apartment. I did not lose hope, three weeks later she gave me the notice that my application for a new apartment was complete and all that was to do is wait a little more. On September 11, 2001, I went to drop off Fernanda in school and then Oswaldo in daycare and then I returned to the shelter and started to feed Natalia, when I heard a very loud noise, I quickly opened the door to my room and saw a lot of people running towards the roof of the shelter. I started to get scared and worried and held Natalia tight, Priscilla came and said that something big had happened that it was a huge fire and that if I wanted to figure out what was going on to go up to the roof, I ran quickly to get myself out of doubts, as I gazed I saw how a plane crashed into one of the twin towers I saw how the tower quickly turned into flames and soon enough black smoke filled the air. I was speechless just like the people around me, I quickly ran to go get my children. When I came back I went back to the roof and held my children with me and as we stared at the twin towers we saw how people would jump of yelling desperate for help, it was an awful sight to watch. Later on we would see one of the towers collapsed and everything turned into smoke we were all shocked everybody was silent we were just staring at the sight, helplessly as sadness seized us all some us started to cry others prayed, It was one of the most difficult moments that will never be forgotten. A few minutes later the second tower collapsed we prayed and stood silent, later we returned to our rooms, the lady who cooked the food had to rush out because her son worked near the World Trade Center so there was no food. Priscilla asked me to help her go buy food for all, in reality almost no one was hungry because of what had happened. After two weeks, I got the news that I was going to get a new apartment, so I set out to look for the apartment I wanted to move into an apartment with my children already I wanted our lives to change, it didn't matter if it was cold or I was hungry I kept on looking, I looked in Brooklyn, Queens, and the Bronx. I finally found an available apartment on October 24 in the Bronx, it was Fernanda's birthday that day we celebrated her birthday in the shelter. Moments like those broke my heart knowing that I could not give my children better not even on their birthdays. Priscilla would always check up on me and give me support when I was about to break down, Thanksgiving came and some friends gave me a turkey but since I had no place to cook it i had to give it away to a lady that worked in the shelter, finally on December 29, Priscilla called me and said "Esperanza I hope you started packing already because you are leaving the refuge and moving into your new apartment you have until January 1st to buy all the furniture you'll need for your new apartment and then you can go back and you take things you have in the shelter",. I almost cried of happiness me and my children were happy and that day I did not send them to school or daycare, and at four in the afternoon the truck came with the things I had bought to leave them in the new house and the things I had in the shelter I would take them later. It was now January 3, the day of my birthday. I started to pack things from the shelter and was determined to move to the Bronx. We left very satisfied and happy I was full of joy and then me and my children arrived in our new apartment, this was truly the best birthday ever for me. Priscilla called me later she was a little upset because I did not let her know that I was leaving and she was planning to celebrate my birthday I told her I appreciated them all, but they had already given me the greatest gift ever my apartment and that I would never forget what she has done for me and my kids she said "Esperanza enjoy your new life with your children and be happy", I thanked her and ended the call as tears ran down my face of happiness.

Chapter 19

We finally were settled in our new home, I had to find a school for Fernanda, and a daycare for Oswaldo. We went to live in the Bronx around 182nd Street near 3rd Avenue. Natalia stayed home with me while Fernanda would go to school and Oswaldo to daycare, a month had gone by fast and I still could not find a job so I decided to contact my old friends and start selling ices again in brooklyn. Before I left to work I would drop off Fernanda and oswaldo in school and then I would leave Natalia with her babysitter. I would go to work around 10 am and return around 5 pm sometimes a little later. That was my daily routine; I would only miss work if I had a doctor appointment for my children or a meeting at school. Four months had gone by I went to work as I always did and like everyday call the lady that would care for my children after school to let her know I would pick up my children soon. Put one particular day I called her I was worried when she answered saying "Esperanza come quick Oswaldo had an accident in his daycare", I asked what had happened and is he okay? She said that he had fallen and broke his nose and also that one of his eye was swollen and looked very bad. I quickly hanged up the phone; the guy that would open the door to leave the carts had not arrived yet, so I left the cart there and asked someone to please give it in for me. I quickly ran to take the train and was very concerned I did not know what had really happened I was panicking, when I arrived the lady that took care of my children quickly said that she had nothing to do with what had happened to Oswaldo and that he had an accident in his daycare I rushed to the hospital seeing my little son crying and barley could open his eye, but when I arrived in the hospital the police were waiting for me, they started to question me as well as the lady who looked after my children, we told them that everything happened in the daycare. They started to investigate and found out it was true that Oswaldo had injured himself in his daycare. Were investigating and they confirmed that the accident was in daycare.

The Police directed me to support center well known as The Puerto Rican Family Institute, I was sent there to take therapies, I was greatly affected by what had happened to Oswaldo it seemed as if life itself made me suffer on purpose. Both me and my children were giving therapy and counseling, that helped us a lot I would take my children out as much as possible to the parks or to eat somewhere. We took like two years of receiving aid from that place, I felt that I also needed help, I did not want my life to fall out of control again. Some coworkers that I worked with while selling ices were family or friends of Martin, so he could find us if he wanted to, I holded a grudge against him even though he was the father of my daughter seeing him will bring me back all the bad memories, I thought that he was to one to blame that because of him me and my children were going through this. One day he showed up, along with her sisters claiming that he came to see Natalia and the other children, I cooked a little something and we all had dinner after that they left, but he showed up the next day he said he wanted to talk to me, so we sat and talked for a long time, according to him he was sorry and that he was a changed man, also that he wanted a second chance. I did not believe a word he said i have heard that a lot before and he never did change. I did not take him back but I allowed him to visit his daughter Natalia.

He would come every three days. Along passed eight months and he came by and proposed that if I would let him live with me and the children, I said okay I'll give you another chance, he did not bring along anything except two pairs of clothes when he moved in. He would barely be home he would go out returning every two or three days. He would give me excuses such as I was working or I stayed over at my sister's house. I really did not care at that point I mostly cared about work and my children, he kept doing what he wanted to do, Christmas was approaching and his brothers wanted us to celebrate, so we started planning to do a feast. On December 24, His brothers and sisters came from New Jersey with their children, I felt very weird and odd. The celebration ended and they left but he stayed. The next morning he got up and went to work, Martin and I had planned to order food on New years and spent as a "New family" that we were, When New year's came along he had not shown up I waited all day and nothing, it was about 10:30pm and I decided to call him, I was surprised when I heard a woman's voice answer the phone, she asked me who was I, I quickly responded "I am the mother of his daughter" and she ended up hanging up the phone on me. Later he called and told me not to wait for him, I responded okay. Three days had passed and he finally showed up he apologized, I asked him who was that woman who answered your phone and he told me it was a friend that he had gone out with some friends and that they were with company I told him "you promised you'll change but it really doesn't matter to me anymore", he smiled and said "forgive me", It's your life and you know what you do with it, after that I went out with the kids and he stayed home, when I came back he was not there anymore. He returned the next day we started talking about Natalia, we wanted to baptize her so that same day we went out to New Jersey to see one of his sisters and ask her and her husband to be the godmother and godfather of Natalia, they agreed and a month later we baptized Natalia. Martin did not change, he still would do the same thing, he would go to work and disappear for days, his family would come often to visit our house in some occasions, one woman also the girlfriend of one of his brothers had just recently come out from Ecuador. Some of Martin's sisters would give him advice and will tell him not to waste the new chance that I had given him. Martin's brother lived in Queens, when Martin didn't show up home he would stay with his brother in queens. Martin's brother started to come over we were planning to celebrate Martins birthday. That day of the celebration, it looked as if Martin and his brother were angry at each other. Later on I found out it was because of money, His brother's girlfriend was coming to the United States and he did not have enough money to pay for her trip. They asked me if they could borrow some money, I had a little saved up but it was for my son Joseph, I could not send it because my mother was upset with me and my sisters too and my son was still a minor. I did not lend them money I didn't trust them at all. Martin called me one night to tell me he was going to look for his brother's girlfriend who had already arrived in New York and that his brother had gotten arrested by immigration. Martin was worried because his brother had presented false papers, and he had been arrested before Martin called me at five in the morning, to tell me that he had picked up his brother's girlfriend. That day I did not go to work, I stay to wait he arrived at about eleven o'clock, Martin told me to help him, he no longer had money and he asked me if I would please lend him some to buy clothes for her. I said okay and went to Queens to buy what she needed. Martin took us in his car; I helped her choose out clothes. Martins brother had gone to prison for seven months and then was deported to Ecuador. While Martins brothers' girlfriend was already here she stayed in martin's brothers' apartment. Martin did not change he would do the same thing he wouldn't come home for days.

Chapter 20

Martin came to the house at times, with the bride's brother. The Queens accompanied her to collect the rent of the rooms of the apartment that had his brother. This had only been able to help him, after which he was deported, and I for one follow selling my ice cream. And in my free time, I started to recycle bottles. One day I went to work earlier, leave the kids at home sleeping, as the lady who looked after them, they would later fetching. I had a feeling. was as if he knew something would happen, but did not know that? It was about twelve noon, when I call home, I was surprised that I answered Fernanda, and even more when I notice that the lady who took care of them even did not come. I asked, passing daughter? And I listened very scared. and I said,! Mommy, there's a fire in the building, and the smoke is getting into, out of windows. I became pale with fright, was about to pass out and not know what to do. My children were alone and did not know what would happen. I phoned the lady who took care of them several times, she replied telling me that he was near the house. It was quiet, I was with this concern, I knew I was going with my children. Then I called back and told me that children were already with her. Stop working and take the train back home. Time just to eternal reach the home of Mrs. and I saw my children, came back to life. The hugged everyone. And gave thanks to God. That day I promised myself I was not going to leave my children alone, no matter what happened, call and quit the job, I started to recycle bottles and cans, but along with the children. Martin did not even notice what had passed. The third day he appeared and told her what happened, but he grinned. I was worried and asked him to help burn some money, such as not cooperating with dela home expenses, due to my situation, I asked him to help with the expenses. But I said nothing.

Just smiled and went, I did not like his reaction, and decided not to say anything, I was harder gridding, recycled in the morning and evening, in those days came the husband of one of my sisters, I took Martin pick it up, went to the airport in New Jersey. he stayed in the house with us. Martin, also stayed longer in the house, so was the man of the house, as the brother was not working, out of desperation, also began to recycle bottles and cans. so was like two months until Martin took him to his work. After about five months, my brother in law decided to move, had decided to go to Long Island. After leaving, Martin was again the same, did not come to the house and made him constantly.Not that I spend? But getting pregnant, did not know until half a pain, when was recycling; Natalia walked with me, I rode in the shopping cart. I did not care, but then felt bad and went to the hospital emergency. Martin was in the house, but he did not care, and went to work, I did some tests and I was surprised when they told me I was pregnant, I did not believe, as I had put a device. The doctors told me that there were two babies, only one was dead and needed to remove it. I did not believe them as I left the hospital, I returned home and went wing to bring the kids to school. . I fed them and so I went to sleep. The next day I went to Manhattan, Martin afternoon and asked me what was? Thinking it would cheer, I told him about my pregnancy. But reacted angrily and I cry!. Have to abort the two, for your sake and mine, I did not think what I heard, so I gave very safe value and I said no. if I was going to have the baby. Ignore it and decided that my baby was born, even risking my health.

I had no money, had not worked and only had two pair travel the train, had sent money Tomy son, Jose. Since he was celebrating his first communion. At the hospital, the doctors told me that my problem was very complicated; I would do a surgery, but no anesthesia. But were concerned because they did not know if I was going to resist and did not want to hurt the other baby. But I told them it was okay if I was strong and from the operating room at about ten in the morning and went out about two o'clock. I was recovering and I was asked to stay because he had lost the baby was a male; they told me they saved to another baby, but assured me that he was born. Only a miracle can help girl, was concerned about the other children. and you call the lady I take care of them. Martin had not gone to pick up and they were still with her. I asked the doctors to let me go to the house, did not want, as it was very weak and very risky. I begged and cried, I was told by my other children who were alone, made me sign some papers to let me out, it was on my own responsibility, what happened to my health. Sali walked up First Avenue, the hospital was on Fifth Avenue and the journey was very long, but on my terms, on occasions had to stop as I was about to faint. I felt exhausted and was weaker. But the concern of my children, I made an effort, as they were waiting for me. Take bus M15 to 125th Street and therefore the BX15 to the Bronx, I had to walk because they were only two that had to travel by bus. I went to bring the kids, the lady I take care of them, I was very weak and worried she offered me to eat, I was dizzy, helped me sit and fed me. After a while she sent her children to us to leave the house, still a little weak, I made a soup for the children because they were hungry. They finished eating and went to sleep. As Martin did not arrive, I started to look for signs of it, the children were already asleep, so I started looking for things that kept her, even though search found nothing, nor the clothes I had, nothing, nothing.

I found a letter, and before opening knew that he had left home. At that moment the phone rang on the doorbell woke Fernanda. It was my friend Laura, she was looking for me, I wanted to know how he was, and we talk a lot for a while and said it was fine, but I knew very well and I believed him! I go to your house, wait, I'm coming!.When I was surprised to see me very weak and emaciated. gave me some advice and was willing to help me, but I saw his gestures was worried about me. She told me, everything will change, do not worry, take forward, encourage. Time had already sold some nutrition products and know how to talk to people, she was taking these products every day and I had brought a bottle of proteins, for me to take and I recovered from the poor health he had. I asked without fail I take that product gave me, tomorrow is another day, I said, that's what it was depues. Fernanda also went to sleep, I had not had time to read this letter, Habri the envelope and started to read it, I said he was leaving home for good, he already had another woman and was going to live with it, was the same with the one I had found him cheating on. I also said that he had seen, that I was a good mother, and not to neglect my children, he knew very well that I never was going to leave. Finally said, not look for me, forget me, I love you not. I started to break the letter, trying to get the courage and anger, as it was possible for me again so cheated and mocked me. lost your mind, pull the pieces of paper and look for a book, start a sheet and started to make a letter, to my friend Laura, asked her, to take care of my children and that after the send, par Ecuador With Me mother I do not seek, as far I would go somewhere else where no longer suffering. I did a farewell letter, I'm just a train trip and wanted to use going to pull the Brooklyn Bridge, to die and end all of a good time. I felt the need to die, I thought I was guilty, I could not mourn over, tired and depressed I was winning, I put the letter under the pillow of Fernanda, take my shoes, to be quiet and go to wake up, I put on my jacket because it was very cold, was about to leave and turned around to see one last time to my children, were asleep, the street light reflected them in the face. Their faces looked like innocent little angels, they did not know what I would do, when he went out to the outside, something stopped me in the middle of the door, I could not cross it, it was like they shouted me that I fuera. Fue something invisible, I think it was God, I would go back and hugged my children, cry and asked forgiveness, God also thanked him for everything he was sorry for what he intended to do. Take the letter he had written and broke.

The next day I continued my life as if nothing had happened, I had promised that no one would suffer, take the kids to school and Natalia stayed with me at home. Clean the house, I wanted to clear my mind to work, it was not easy for me, the bad thoughts took possession of me, was angry with life, with all that I had lived. But I had two choices, complain about everything or be strong and move forward. Days later, my friend Laura called me, asking if I had taken the products that leave me, wanted to know how I felt and if he had any reaction. I told him if he was taking, but he had not felt anything and I did not pay attention. I realized my health and energy, only until she asked me. Follow him taking me said, you will help a lot. Certainly the doctors had told me to be careful, if I wanted my baby to be born. How could it work like that before, my friend Laura suggested I do the same to her, recommend products that I took. She would help me gain a discount, accept, but still recycling, so I started selling nutrition products. Used the time and spend more time with my children, went out to the park or walk, we enjoyed and we had fun together. Gradually, I found people interested in the products and I felt so happy to help others in my new job I was happy and could also help many more.

Chapter 21

My joy was that my pregnancy was going very well, thanks to drinking those products I started to gain a little more money, thanks to new customers and friend. I would still Recycle; I also started to talk to my son and my mother, our communication improved by little, but sometimes I would avoid calling them because I knew they were angry at me because of my sister's Rocio comments, her husband who was in New York as well would always call Rocio to tell his stories about what me and children went through but he would always tell it his way. Almost always he made me look ridiculous in front of my mother and son. Christmas was approaching and wanted to save a little, but I couldn't because I had to pay for electricity, telephone and food costs. My children began to help me recycle, for me and my children Christmas was like any other regular day. On day a lady saw us recycling and saw my children helping me, she approached us very friendly and invited us to a place where they gave away toys to children. So we attended the place, they had no toys but they gave us food, we also got an invitation for the 25 of December so the kids can get gifts. The only problem was that it was at night and it would be cold and snowing, I told them that I was worried of my children getting sick they offered to pick us up from my house to the place, I accepted because I had no money to buy my children gifts, I thought at least for them it will be a happy Christmas. New year's came along and I spent it at home with my children, while everybody celebrated I was sad I missed my son and my mother in Ecuador, I called them to wish them a happy new year my mother picked up the phone and told me that my son Jose was mad at me, she kept talking to me through the phone and she asked me if I'm living alone with my children, I told her yes and she said that it is better like that and to keep it up and stay strong for my kids. It was February and I wasn't feeling well but I kept on working, the little that I kept earning from selling the products I would keep saving to buy the necessary things my baby would need when it was born. Although my situation was hard one happiness kept me going and that was that my baby would be born healthy and good thanks to the products I was drinking. Time had gone by quick, on February 19 at about four in the afternoon Martin came knocking on the door furious and threw an envelope with money at me while I layed in bed, he had told me that his sisters had forced him to come, he insulted me and told me that the reason he left me money was so I would stop bothering him, he rushed out in rage and i got up and took the envelope of money and followed him out and threw the envelope at his head and yelled "I do not need any charity from you!, take your money!". he picked up the envelope and left without saying a word, I went back inside and I started to feel very bad so I called a friend that was also my neighbor and asked her to accompany me to the hospital, I left my children with a lady that lived below me. My baby wasn't supposed to be born now she was planned to be born in couple of more months. When I got the hospital the doctors asked me what had happened and I told them the issue that had occurred with Martin, the doctors started to check me and see how my baby was doing I was complaining of pain and my belly was hard as rock I was scared of what might happen advancement birth, arrived at the hospital and asked, what had happened, I had to say what had happened, I kept on asking the doctors if my baby was gonna be okay they said yes but we have to do section. At around 4 am February 20 my baby girl was born, I decided to call her Luz. when I saw her for the first time she was so small she weighed only three pounds and two ounces and was born premature only seven months. But she was perfectly healthy. The doctors took me to a room so I can recuperate. I was left alone, although I had a great joy because my baby was born I was also sad because I would see other mothers with their husbands and family and I had no one beside me. I felt powerless, insignificant. I called my neighbor to check up on my children and see if they were okay, they were good I got to talk to them and they asked me if the baby was born yet. They jumped of joy when I told them yes and I also told them that she was okay and healthy. I was left alone with the baby and the next day I called check up on my children again but to my surprise nobody picked up the phone I got a little worried. Later on like around 1:30pm, I was surprised to see my children and my neighbor they came to visit me in the hospital, I cried of joy and from that moment on I realized that God had sent me these wonderful children, I hugged them and told them thank you for visiting me and to behave they said yes mommy. Fernanda told me "mommy we will be waiting for you and our baby sister at home", I was kept almost a week in the hospital, I wanted to go home already. I was desperate and I asked a nurse when were they going to let me go home, she told me that they were waiting on some results and then they would let me know if I could go home or not. Later on the nurse came along and said that I could go home but I needed someone to pick me up because I was still too weak from my operation. I did not know who to ask, so I called Martin's sister who lived in New Jersey I told her to do me a big favor and come pick me up from the hospital but she couldn't because she was working. I had to call Natalia godmother which was the other sister of Martin she told me that her and her husband will come pick me up but a little later because her husband was still working. It was about six in the afternoon when they arrived, Natalia's godmother came first and her husband stood downstairs parking the car because it was snowing, they gave me a baby basket to carry the baby in, I cried with excitement and thanked them for helping me. When we got home, the kids were happy they jumped of excitement and wanted to see their baby sister. Natalias godfather asked me where was the baby gonna sleep, very sad I said I did not have a crib for the baby because I was not expecting it to come so soon. He said he would go out and look for crib for

Luz I gave him a money and he left. When he finally returned, later came the other sister of Martin with her husband, they had brought clothes and a bathtub for Luz, they stayed over and helped cook for my children after we had dinner they left back to New Jersey, again I was alone I spent three days in bed recuperating, and then i noticed that my children had no clean clothes so I had to go do laundry. But first I had to wait for the pediatrician who would come to the house and check up on Luz and me, everything had gone well my wound was healing right from the C-section I had to go through, the pediatrician had ordered me to rest and take care of myself because if I did a lot my wound could open. When the pediatrician left i also left slowly towards the Laundromat, I lived on the fifth floor and there was no elevator, I had two sack of laundry, so first I would take the baby down and children would follow me, then I would have to go back up for the sacks of clothes only Fernanda would help me because she was the oldest, they pushed the stroller and I took the sacks of clothes in the shopping cart, the Laundromat was about three or four blocks away, when I finished laundry I went back home I took the children up first then went back for the clothes as I was going up with the cart I felt that I out too much strength and felt a sharp pain in my wound, I finished bring up the cart and checked my wound, it had opened my kids started crying because they saw I was in pain. I tried to calm them down and called the hospital they gave me instructions and in 40 minutes they send a nurse to my house. The nurse cleaned and sowed my wound and ordered me to rest for various days, the nurse would come every two days to check up on me and the baby, the only thing I was allowed to do was cook for my children. The little money that I had was gone and I had to go outside with the magazine of products and start to talk to people and offer the products, I would sell but it wasn't enough for me so again I started to recycle and that helped me get out of the situation I was in for a while.

Chapter 22

It was a very difficult time, but I had to find a way to keep moving forward, my children only depended on me. My everyday job was recycling after I would leave my kids at school sometimes I would go recycle at night when my kids fell asleep. I also started recommending the products to people, one day I felt a really strong pain in my right arm, and as each day past the pain would get more sever. I went to the hospital, but the doctors told me that they found nothing wrong and they could not explain where the pain was coming from. There only solution was to give me pain relievers. About two weeks later, Natalia also started to feel pain in her arm, i could go through the pain but my daughter no, we both had pain in the same right arm , the pain was unbearable we would both end in eh floor crying, later on we both noticed that in our right arm we saw a black bruise that kept getting bigger every day. We consulted several doctors and several hospitals no one could help us, we wanted that pain to disappear, so I called a nephew who lived in Queens, with Don Rodolfo and Mrs. Bernarda ,Desperate I told him what was happening he said "aunt come to here, we can help you better here," I told the kids to pack some clothes and we left, they gave us a small place in his room to stay, there, Don Rodolfo and Mrs. Bernarda also lived, they asked what was wrong ? And all I could say is I didn't know but I was desperate to find out, they told me to go to the hospital in Flushing, in Queens. I went alone with Natalia, the other children I left behind with their grandparents to babysit, as me and Natalia were walking towards the hospital we came upon a sharp pain, we stopped against a wall crying of the pain we were in, a person who was passing asked if we were okay? Since she saw us crying, she helped us walk to the hospital. As soon as we got to the hospital the doctors began to check us they made us studies, and we had to wait for a few hours, they started to ask if we had gone to different hospitals or doctors, I said yes but all the doctors gave me the same answer and that was that they don't find nothing wrong with my arm and that they can't explain why was I having pain and where did it come from. And to my surprise they told me the same thing that they didn't know where the pain was coming from but they saw that both our arms had a black bruise, they thought I was a strange sickness and they suggested that they should amputate our arms before it spreads to our body. I quickly said NO I would not allow them to cut mines or my child's arm and I quickly left the hospital with Natalia. We walked a little and stopped a moment, people looked at us as the two of us cried in pain and despair. A woman came over and asked what was wrong? Crying I told her what was happening to us, very quiet she said, "have a lot of faith woman, In this life there are many good things and also bad evil hurts some people believe it or not! LOOK! I'll give you the address of a person who can help you, go and see her, she'll help, she is very good with these cases. That confuses me a bit, I went back to the apartment of my nephew arriving there they asked us how was everything I told them what had happened, after a while I told Mrs. Bernarda what had happened with the woman that gave me an address, we ate a bit and after that I rushed to look for the address.

Natalia and I were increasingly getting worse, I thought to myself I would not give up and imma do anything it takes to cure me and child, I finally had found the address when I knocked on the door a lady came out and walked us in her house. We told her what happened and despair that we had and pain, she started to check our arms and said come back later because she was a little busy with other people. I told her that we would wait for the time necessary and she said then to have a seat and wait while she assisted the other people. Twenty minutes went by and Natalia had a severe pain in her arm, the lady heard the screams and came out fast and gave us water and Tylenol to calm some of the pain. We waited for two hours until she finally was done with the other people, she started to ask us questions and she asked me "do you believe in God?" I said yes and she told me you have to have a lot of faith I'm going to pray for you so you and your daughter can get better and then she asked me "are you devoted to any specific saint?" I quickly told her the Divine Child Jesus i started to pray but with a lot of faith. The lady began to pray, and took Natalia's by the arm she lifted her little by little, and she began moving her more and more, Natalia lost consciousness and fell asleep for a while and the lady woke her, it was amazing! When she woke up Natalia looked perfectly fine and she said that he did not hurt. Then she did the same to me, she raised my arm while praying, I felt the pain was disappearing and the I could move my arm slowly. the only thing I felt was sleepy, she told me everything would be okay and that me and Natalia were okay and we may go home but must return tomorrow because she must do several sessions to cure me and Natalia, I asked her how much would it be and she said $ 1500.00 dollars, I had no money at the time but she told me not to worry for now. I asked my nephew if he would do me the favor of lending me money, he agreed and then I took all of the money I have saved from the products I sold, the next day the lady told me that what me and Natalia had was very delicate and that the session would last about a month, so I stayed with my nephew and with the grandparents of Fernanda and Oswaldo. Mrs. Bernarda would help me tie and comb my hair, she helped me with my children, and she also helped me cook. A month later we returned back home to the Bronx, we were very happy to return home, the nightmare was over and me and my daughter were healed, our arms were better now, my only concern now was that all the money that I had was finished, but I had faith that we would move forward again, with God's grace.

Chapter 23

Thanks to those who I had as clients drinking the nutrition product earned some money it was not much but it helped me a lot. With that I had a motive to go out and look for more customers by selling these products I helped people improve their health and I also helped myself economically. I was very attentive of my children but I would use the free times that I had to recommend the products. My good friend Laura saw how hard I was trying to prosper that she invited me to this seminar meeting about the products, I liked learning about nutrition and helping others, also I was very grateful because my daughter Luz was born healthy because of the product. I started to attend my therapies and seminars about the products and company. My mentality started to change my mind started to open to more dreams, to seek a better quality of life, Laura told me "Esperanza, this business is yours and since you are your own boss your job is to make it prosper and succeed, I got to know many people, who later I became friends with, I had many customers but one of them had an incredible result with the products. He was a very overweight man, he had gone through a heart attack and survived, he was an alcoholic he was also diabetic and weighed 297 lbs. He was losing a lot of weight and improving his health, I wanted to help him too and suggested that he do the same as me and recommend the products with the people he knew, he did not accept at first but I invited to the seminar I was going to and it changed his opinion, the reason he agreed is because he wanted to help his family who also were diabetic and were overweight, so he also began his business. I sometimes had few sales and did not have enough money for my bills. I began to invite people to my house so I could show them samples of the product I started working from home, people came and went, one day some people came invited by some of my customers they had just arrived from a trip as they had some suitcases with them, after a few days from visiting the house they left. One morning my daughter Natalia felt something had bitten her in the foot, I quickly checked around her leg and I saw an animal they were called bed bugs, that day I ignored it, days after my other children also had got bitten by bedbugs, I started to spray the house, I did not know that my children had placed their school bags in the same place that the visitor's placed their suitcases also my kids left their toys and some stuffed animals near the suitcases, My children would get fever and they were always itchy when those animals would bite them, I started to worry and went to report the problem to the office so they would fumigate the apartment I thought they would help me but they didn't. A couple of days later the owner of the building came over and was very angry at me and accused me of infesting the building with bed bugs. The lady only spoke English, she started to say so many things to me that I could not understand, so I would ask the super of the building to translate for me. The lady told me that the bed bugs were all over the building, the super told me that he had reported that there was a case of bed bugs about a month ago but the landlord did not do anything about it, she left very angry and upset, I did not know that the building already had that problem. The neighbor who had witnessed the discussion suggested I call the city and make a complaint; I did not want trouble and decided to wait until they fix the problem but as time passed they didn't do anything for the problem, but to my surprise the lady who was in charge of the building reported me first and defamed me, and accused me that I gathered furniture from the trash inside the building and that I was the one to blame for the building being infested. I decided to call my social worker and tell her everything that was going on. I had to send the bills of the furniture I had bought to prove that I did not gather them from the trash. I asked for help in many places, but my kids were afraid, because the woman had sworn to me that she would kick me out of the building. Days later, she appeared in the building with the super and told me that she was going to kick me off my apartment and that she had already told the city officials and they approved her decision she also made fun of my immigration status, she kept insulting me and disrespecting me for causing so much trouble.

My children were coming from school, and I could not avoid for them to hear what was going on and how was the lady treating me, my children were frightened that we were gonna get kicked out our home, Fernanda got depressed the most and a few days after Fernanda fainted I quickly took her to the hospital and there I found out that she had a murmur on her heart, she had that problem a very long time ago since she was little, when Rosendo had abandoned us, now that problem had come back and I didn't know what to do the doctors told me that Fernanda need care and that any hard emotion can be dangerous. She was under care for two weeks and was put a heart monitor so the doctors can keep track on she was doing. For worrying about Fernanda I have forgotten about the apartment problems when I had gone to check my mailbox I found a letter that stated that I must leave the apartment, but because I was focusing on my daughter when I noticed I only had 24 hours to leave the apartment .

That same day of me finding out the owner came with the super and started to pack my stuff in big black trash bags and started to throw them away. My children were crying they were scared; the woman was walking through the house shouting in English she was not sorry for my children, the children cried seeing them empty the closets, seeing them throw our clothes away in garbage bags and also toys. We were left with nothing, desperate I called Carlos, he had moved near where we lived and worked there starting to sell products and recommending it, I asked him to help us out and let me and my children stay at his house. He agreed, I had to stay wait for the city to review my case. We stayed in Carlos house for a month or so and finally I got the notice from the city letting me know I could look for an apartment and after two weeks I moved to an apartment one block away from where Carlos lived, and my children moved. I had no money because I have not been working, I only had a few things and the image of the Divine Child who always accompanied us. In my children's school the teachers already knew about our situation, and two of them were kind enough to help us. One of the teachers gave Fernanda a bed and another teacher gave us a sofa and dishes, I was very thankful and appreciated what they I had done for us. We were going through a hard time and my children were getting very distracted from school so much that there grades reflected it, I decided to sit down with them and talk and explain to them that everything was gonna be okay and that they have to focus on school work and i will deal with everything they said okay mommy and started studying and doing homework. I had to go to my old job of recycling in the morning and evening and during the day I will recommended the nutrition products. Carlos lived nearby and we would often go out together to find new customers to sell products too, I kept in my mind what I had learned in the seminars that dreams do come true, and I am going to make my dreams come true for my kids. Because of all the problems me and my children were going threw i didn't pay attention to my health and I started to get sharp pain in my stomach, I could barely eat because my stomach would inflamed, I did not say anything because I did not want to worry my children, but Carlos realized and I had to tell him the truth. but it. One night I felt the pain so sharp that I could not sleep the children were frightened and called 911 for them to send an ambulance they also called Carlos to tell him what was going on, when the ambulance arrived they took me to the hospital, Carlos went to the house first in the house was Alejandro a good friend of the family who was visiting, Carlos decided to go to the hospital and check up on me while Alejandro stayed home with my children. When I got to the hospital the doctors did a lot of studies on me and I stayed for observation the whole night, the next day they told me that I had nothing wrong and send me home. They had prescribed me medicine that I could not buy but not because I didn't want to but because it was too much money and I had barely enough to pay for the house bills and worry about my children. I kept on with the pain but I did not let my kids see me like that, I kept on drinking the products and recommending it, but again I felt bad so I had to call the ambulance but like before they didn't find anything wrong with me. Until I had a high fever that I could not walk, I felt very weak, and I kept drinking the products and I will feel better that was like my only pain killer. I did not feel the same force, I was unwilling and powerless, at night I could not sleep because of I was in so much pain in my stomach, it would inflamed so I would have to take laxatives, I stayed at home for several days, thinking I was going to get better, I could no longer work I was in so much pain and desperate I ordered Fernanda to call the ambulance. The paramedics stabilized me and asked me which hospital I wanted to go, I asked them to take me to Montefiore hospital, I stayed there two nights and one day and after that the doctors asked me to return to do other studies. So I went back to see my results and the doctors tell me they had found something in my stomach and it was a tumor and they recommended me that I had to have surgery as soon as possible, they scared me but I put myself in their hands so they can do what was necessary to cure me, I did not know what was going to happen, I thought what would happen if something went wrong?. I went through treatment first and then I had a colposcopy. The doctors removed the tumor without a problem everything went very well with the first surgery. When I was in recovery and the doctors were surprised because the tumor that they had removed was in my stomach for about 8 years and it had not grown a lot like it did in other people who had the same thing as me, they asked what have done to keep it that little because for someone else they would have been dead by now. Since I was still under anesthesia I could not speak very well, so they had called Carlos and Carlos explained that we were drinking nutrition products, they were surprised and told me to keep on drinking whatever I was drinking because it helped me a lot. I continued consuming the products and thanks to the products I recovered fast. Again I returned and was waiting for whatever else the future had for me.

Chapter 24

 arlos kept on working in what I was working, he rented a room to two people and we started to work as a team giving samples of the products. We both had our own clients and after some time, on a Sunday morning Carlos had gone to Manhattan to a special seminar and I had gone to my house. When Carlos had come back he had gone to visit us first and from there we walked him home because we were supposed to pick up some products, when we got there we noticed that the door was opened we quickly rushed upstairs to see what was going on, when we got upstairs we saw stuff on the floor and the stereo system was gone also two boxes full of product that carlos had received, carlos quickly ran towards his room and noticed that it was busted opened he was concerned about some money that he kept in his drawer but when he checked it wasn't there along with that the thieves stole dvd's, cd's, jewelry, personal documents, the money saved up to pay the rent and also the money of sold product. Seeing all of this i called the police, they arrived after 20 minutes they asked several questions and I had to explain what had happened because Carlos was angry and furious, the police told us that they were going to investigate and then gave us a report and left after that. Me and my children told Carlos to come stay in our house because what would happen if by any chance they would come back. The next day we told the owner of the house but he said he could not do anything about it, the apartment lease had expired and we wanted to renew the lease but the owner refused because of the incident he only gave us one month to vacate their apartment, we had to talk to people that would visit us and consume the products because some of the people had ordered products and we could not give it to them because of the robbery, some were upset with us and accused us of stealing we asked for time and showed them the police report to get out of this situation we borrowed money. Carlos was disappointed and had low energy and had lost the will to continue the business, so he went to look for work in a fruit place in order to pay back the money we now owed. I wanted to keep working at home but I did not have a place to put the business running. Carlos moved to another place but he usually would still come and visit us. On one occasion the owner had come by to collect the rent and I decided to ask him if he gave me permission to work in the house I had to explain to him that I was recommending and selling products and that people would come to my house and consume it in the mornings and the afternoon, he agreed and so I started to invite people and little by little more and more people started coming I could no longer alone. I decided to invite Carlos to see if he would help me, at first I didn't want to because he was still upset about what had happened with the whole robbery situation but then later on he changed his mind, we started working again as a team. One day the owner surprised us and said that he liked our business he was such a nice person and offered us the basement to work in. Although the basement was in poor conditions I accepted it because I thought it was the best, the owner gave us permission to repair it. Carlos and I took advantage of our free time to clean and renovate the basement, so we could start working as a team and be able to pay the debt that had already been increased. Carlos decided to move downstairs in the basement for to be much easier to him, we split the work and took turns to look assist the people that would come and consume and then we would go visit our on clients. We both were eager to get out of the horrible economic situation

Chapter 25

We were in My job was not me enough to pay the expenses and we still had debts, also I had problems with the help they gave me from the city because many times they would close my case and then reopen it, I did not understand why. Natalia started to get sick all the time and I had to always find a way to pay the bills and care for them and on top of that I had no more help from the city because they closed my case, I would go to churches and collect food but I was not going to let my children starve or go hungry, I tried to reopen my case but they told me I had to wait. It broke my heart seeing Lucesita and Natalia going up to the fridge to look for something to eat and then not finding anything. We all suffered, but

Natalia was affected more by this situation because one morning as I told my children to get up for school I noticed Natalia looked a little pail I asked her if she was okay and she said no that she felt sick and asked me to stay home, I allowed it and told her to rest but during the day she became very ill and started to get a high fever also she had trouble breathing and could barely move. I quickly took her to the hospital but there were so many people we had to wait, as we waited i noticed that Natalia was getting worse and she could not breath I yelled for a nurse to help me. The nurse ran and immediately called a doctor so she can be admitted, one of the nurses told me that Natalia had just had a asthma attack, the doctors put oxygen on her, I did not know my daughter suffered from asthma I stayed in the hospital that day and would see doctors coming in and out of the room checking up on my daughter, it hurt a lot to see my daughter so helpless and sick. My other children also were concerned, Natalia was in the hospital for about a week or so and then the doctors said she could go home, everyone was very happy to see her again especially Luz since they both always played and they loved each other very much. After a while like a month or so I went back to the hospital but this time it was for Luz, since the cold had begun Luz got very sick because the change of weather, she had the same health problem as Natalia so I decided not to send her to school. When I took her to the hospital the doctors decided to keep her admitted. I started to get really worried because Luz was premature and they were very delicate children to take care of, I stood in the hospital with Luz for three days until the doctor said she could finally go home. This whole situation was affecting my children very badly I noticed that there grades in school were dropping so I decided to sit down and talk to them they had to learn to be positive no matter what happens we started talking and started remembering all we'd been through, I told them that we had to be strong and that I was going to look for help again they said "Mom, go to Puerto Rican Program". The fact was that we were going through a difficult time and every time I would feel worse about myself, I started to despise men and thought that it was their fault that we were going through this I wished I had never known them. I called the center support Puerto Rican Program but nobody answered, I waited a couple of weeks and I called again I thought that luck was on my side when I heard someone answer the phone. I explained to them that I would like to be involved in their program again, that Oswaldo and Fernanda were already adolescence and sometimes I could not control I told them I was afraid that one day I make a stupid move and take my kids through a bad path. That's precisely the reason why I seek help so they could help me on how to guide them; I have been father and mother to them. I will move ahead with my children, despite the fact that life will treat me that way, I decided to live life to the fullest, and enjoy every moment along with my children.

Chapter 26

I'm having problems with my eyes but I do not say anything to my children, I cannot stand the light of day and Fernanda and Oswaldo started asking me what was wrong I said it's nothing from them not to worry, but they would insist that I made a eye doctors appointment I would keep on telling them that I will later on but I never did. One day I took Natalia to her dentist's appointment and while we were waiting for her to be called I started to feel dizzy and the light started bothering me a lot, Natalia realized and asked what was wrong and I told her that I was okay but again she insisted for me to make a doctor's appointment. So afterwards I went to make an appointment in the eye clinic after

I made the appointment Natalia got so happy from that day Natalia counted down the days for my eye appointment. Until the day finally arrived, I was worried because I did not know what the doctors were going to say, we both arrived at the hospital to check in and waited for awhile so they can call us in. As we waited two doctors approached us and called us in one of them took Natalia and I went into the other room with my doctor I left the door semi opened so when Natalia was finished she could come in, the doctor after a revisions explained what I had she told me that unfortunately what I had was bad and advanced she told me that I had a sickness that had no cure for my eyes she also told me that as time went by I would lose my site and go blind, At the moment Natalia walked in and had heard the doctor tell me that I was going to go blind She quickly yelled "blind! my mom is going to go blind?" for a moment me and the doctor stood silent and after she started explaining to Natalia what was my sickness about. For me the world was over I wanted to die, I looked at Natalia and saw her crying she had not accepted what she had heard. I left crying and asked Natalia not to say anything when we would get home but her pain was too big that when we got home she couldn't resist but crying, Oswaldo and Fernanda asked Natalia what was wrong, why was she crying, I still was in shock and I would only think why me?. Natalia had already told them what had happened and Oswaldo and Fernanda asked me "is it true" with a knot in their throat hoping that I would say no it's not true but I told them yes. Natalia and I told them what the doctor had explained to us, as we explained they cried and cried and told me that everything was going to be okay and that together we'll find a way to overcome this. At the end we all hugged and I thought what a great family I have, that night everybody went to bed except me I stood up the whole night and asked myself why me and what was going to happen with my life when I go blind. Many questions were going through my head at that moment but that's when I realized that not everything is work that I have to enjoy my children while I still can. Morning came and I asked Fernanda to go out with me since we never been out together only the two of us she agreed happily and we went to Manhattan, I just wanted to go out and walk to clear my mind off everything me and Fernanda were talking on the way, I wanted to believe everything was dream that I still haven't woken up from, there were times I did not accept what I was diagnosed with. My other children stayed home I had asked Carlos to please care for them a while since he spent all the time home because he lived and worked in the basement, he agreed to take care of them. I wanted to be away I did not want my children to see me suffer. After that I decided to consult with other doctors and see if they have a different opinion but everyone told me the same thing but I did not lose faith I gripped of God. My children looked sad, and I decided to seek help again, I want them to be prepared for what will happen so I returned to Puerto Rican Program Institute and there I found two angels, they had patience to listen to my problems and thanks to that I have gone ahead with my children and personally motivate me a lot, so I consider them my angels. I cannot work as before, I daylight bothers my eyes, I' go to get food in churches but also try to help people around me recommending the nutrition products and now I spend more time with my children and I enjoy every moment in life with them, In the mornings I thank God for the blessings he gives me. I actually wrote this book as a self therapy and with the support of Puerto Rican Program for the therapies I received from them and also helping me to share my story, so we can help as many women as possible with the same problems I went through. I say indeed it was not easy sharing my story it still hurts remembering my past and I start to cry every time I remember. I've learned that things happen for something good but it depends on you, I live my life everyday like it was my last day living and that's how you should live yours, I'm a human like you, just read my story, often you cannot deal with your problems alone, it's better to find the right help. Often we deceive ourselves thinking we are smart enough to get out of any situation we are afraid to ask for help and to think that we are weak or fearful, I asked for help and believe me that my family and I are so far thankful with what we have experienced because we know it happened for a reason. We have learned a lot as a family, we have fallen as a family and we still keep fighting and be strong and united as a family. A lot of the time being strong doesn't mean you have to face your problems by yourself it means looking for help that's what makes you stronger. In my case, the doctors tell me there is no cure for my disease, but I leave myself up to God only he knows why he is doing this to me and I accept it. I know that if I find the means to cure myself I will continue to fight for my dreams as always and I will continue sharing my story because I would like to help someone avoid the mistakes I made or motivate them. I have learned that if you want something you can have it, because it doesn't matter where you are what matters is where you want to go from there. My actions are the result of now I'm living, but I made the decision to change it, so I wrote this book as a legacy for my children, so they have an idea of what life is like for some people.

It's my first book and I would love for it not to be the last, I hope you liked it and share it. I decided to live my life every moment because of all the suffering, and sorrow and that made me stronger.

End

CRUZ Patino

cruzpatino27 @ yahoo.com
347 - 340 - 4214
347 - 726 - 3964

CPSIA information can be obtained
at www.ICGtesting.com
Printed in the USA
FFOW02n1812020315
11509FF